# The Roman Forum

WEIDENFELD AND NICOLSON  5 WINSLEY STREET  LONDON W1

# Michael Grant    The Roman Forum

PHOTOGRAPHS BY WERNER FORMAN

SBN 297 00199 X

Designed by Gerald Cinamon
for George Weidenfeld and Nicolson Ltd, London
Maps and plans drawn by Claus Henning

Phototypeset by Keyspools Ltd, Golborne, Lancs
Printed by Arnoldo Mondadori, Verona

Endpaper: *Campo Vaccino* after Piranesi,
courtesy: Victoria and Albert Museum.

# Contents

# The Forum Since the End of Antiquity

# Foreword

We owe so much, good and bad, to Rome, that incomparable city which has remained continuously important for longer than any other. The heart of ancient Rome was the Forum. It has been rightly described as the most famous meeting place in the world, and in all history. No other equally small area has seen such a multiplicity of happenings. We know the Forum from what the Romans wrote; and its mass of ruins spreading over the ground is one of the most imposing testimonies that antiquity has handed down to us. They are enormous yet fragmentary, crammed with history but very confusing. This book is an attempt to find a way through these remains, to discover what is important in them, and to explain their grandeur and significance.

I have adopted, on the whole, a concrete approach. This may sound like a bad pun, since one of the most bewildering features of the area today consists of enormous heaps of derelict-looking concrete – that wonderful material which enabled the Romans to eclipse the Greeks in architectural boldness but which was never intended to be seen. However, I mean the point in a more general sense. Before anything useful can be said about the Forum, the first necessity is to show what the monuments were like.

I shall try to build up this picture not so much from evocations of what has vanished but from what is actually visible today. The central portion of the book, Part 2, is devoted to this task. In each of its sections I shall say something about the role the various monuments fulfilled in the life of the Forum and of Rome, and I shall indicate some of the events associated with them. But before doing this I propose to offer, in the first part, a general survey of the significance of the Forum. At the end I shall add an account of its fate during the centuries after ancient Rome had vanished.

Like any other student of the subject, I owe an enormous debt to the archaeologists who have progressively brought the ancient Forum before our eyes. A few of their works are listed at the end. I also want to thank Mr John Fleming and Mr Hugh Honour for suggestions regarding the last part of the book. I am grateful to Mrs Sandra Bance of George Weidenfeld and Nicolson Ltd for much editorial assistance, to Miss Sabine Oswalt for making a number of helpful suggestions, to Mr Werner Forman for taking most of the photographs, and to my wife for her excellent advice and other assistance of very many kinds.

MICHAEL GRANT
*Gattaiola, 1970*

# Part I

# The Centre of the World

# 1. The Life of the Forum

## WHAT HAPPENED IN THE FORUM

The whole population of Rome's vast empire looked in the direction of the Forum – and all who could do so made their way towards this narrow space, to swell the enormous, loquacious, volatile crowds that congregated there. This was the greatest of what Lord (Sir Kenneth) Clark called 'the open squares of Latin civilization, with their resistant masonry echoing the shouts of uninhibited extroversion'. Here was the nucleus of the business and commercial affairs of the empire. The buildings surrounding the small open rectangle were the centres of government life, where elections were conducted and public notices posted and where every sort of political happening occurred.

Above all, this was the place of speeches, delivered from many a platform, tribunal, basilica and temple. Oratory in the ancient world was a part of life several thousand times more important than it is now, and above all it dominated the Roman Republic and exercised an immense power for good and ill. Orators had to compete with one another in the Forum before a number of equally exacting but otherwise very different audiences: the Assembly, the Senate, and the courts which gave the world Rome's supreme contribution, its law. Before all these gatherings Cicero delivered the supreme masterpieces which have come down to us today.

Often he spoke in crisis conditions; for those last years of the failing Republic were a time when the Forum witnessed almost continuous outbreaks of bloody scuffling. When he defended the gangster Milo (52 BC) on the charge of murdering his fellow-gangster Clodius – whom Cicero hated above all other politicians – the scene was a lurid one. The cremation of Clodius by a hysterical mob had caused such devastation that the Senate-house was destroyed by fire. All the shops – those that survived – were shut, and Pompey, on whom national order depended, was present nearby with picked troops; indeed the entire Forum was packed with soldiers. For once, at the sight of weapons flashing on all sides, the flow of Cicero's eloquence became somewhat thin.

This was the place, eight years later, where the body of Julius Caesar was burnt by vast excited crowds, and where Antony delivered the funeral speech that Shakespeare has imagined and immortalized. Subsequently, Antony and his fellow-triumvirs published here the proscriptions which proclaimed the impending deaths of their political victims, including Cicero. When Sulla, earlier in the century, had embarked on similar proscriptions, it was in the Forum that he sold the victims' property by auction; and this gruesome custom continued.

Yet here, also, was the sacred home of the solemn religious life that was so indissolubly associated with all the official activities of Rome. The leaders of the nation spared no pains in urging the people to perform the traditional observances with patriotic care. All the most important sacrifices were executed in these revered shrines, and during times of emergency all eyes were turned on such rituals in profound anxiety and hope.

The figure of Victory: part of a relief (second century AD) of Victory and Apollo which originally decorated the Basilica Aemilia; now in the Forum Museum.

A peculiar function of the Forum, recurrent with a good deal of frequency owing to the Roman taste for conquest, was to serve as the scene and route of the triumphal processions of generals.

After entering the city by the western Triumphal Gate (Porta Triumphalis), the victorious commander and his troops circled the Palatine Hill and moved down the Sacred Way to the Forum, from which they proceeded up to Jupiter's Temple on the adjacent Capitol. In 46 BC people saw the astonishing spectacle of the fifty-four-year-old Julius Caesar climbing up the steep pavement of the Capitoline Rise on his knees. The incident shows the continuing power of superstition, not perhaps in Caesar who lacked belief in such things, but in the hearts of the Roman population as a whole. For the axle-tree of his chariot had broken during the first of his four processions, and he was thrown onto the ground. Triumphs habitually included various rites intended to ward off evil. Now, after such an unfavourable omen, Caesar decided to add to them by this uncomfortable atonement. He performed the ordeal by torchlight, while forty men bearing lamps rode on elephants to his right and left.[1]

When the Emperor Claudius celebrated a Triumph for the conquest of Britain (AD 44), he decided to repeat Caesar's kneeling pilgrimage. Though the same age as his illustrious predecessor, Claudius was singularly unathletic, and had to be held up by two court officials as he crawled on his way.[2]

Claudius' son Nero performed an astonishing variant of the traditional Triumph when he celebrated victories he had gained not on the field of battle but in the athletic and musical festivals of Greece. Clad in a purple robe, wrapped in a cloak glittering with gold stars, crowned by the wild olive of the Olympic Games and brandishing the bay-leaves of their Pythian counterpart at Delphi, the emperor, with the distinguished harpist Diodorus at his side, rode in a golden chariot down the Sacred Way to the Forum, hailed by the crowds as the only national conqueror since the beginning of all time. Then he duly moved up to the Capitol. But this time the final destination was not Jupiter's Capitoline temple. Instead it was to be the shrine of Apollo, patron of the arts, upon the adjacent Palatine Hill: and it was to Apollo, there, that he dedicated the 1,808 crowns he had won for his performances in Greece. Conservatives were desperately shocked by the whole proceedings.

Triumphs terminated in huge banquets in the Forum. And the celebrations on such occasions, and at funerals too, included lethal contests between gladiators. The Forum had long served as a place for the execution of condemned criminals, and from 216 BC the custom was extended to the staging of gladiatorial 'Games'.[3] This institution, which may have originated from the practices of the Etruscans, meant that Italian forums had to be planned differently from Greek town centres. The need to provide for gladiatorial shows may account for narrow underground galleries and rooms in the centre of the Roman Forum (dating in their present form from about the first century BC). For to judge from marks on the walls and vaults of these chambers, and from the remains of wooden installations, this honeycomb of subterranean structures may have been used for windlasses designed to hoist the contestants to ground level.[4] This would have been particularly useful for wild beast shows. Augustus boasted he had given twenty-six of these displays, totalling a massacre of 3,500 animals,[5] and the Forum was the scene of a considerable proportion of the slaughter.

To meet the needs of such occasions, the whole area was sometimes roofed with awnings. For the unprecedented series of entertainments accompanying his Triumphs, Caesar covered the entire Forum in this

Terracotta relief, originally painted,
of Victory sacrificing a bull; a popular theme in
Greek and Roman art. Forum Museum.

way, as well as the streets leading into it. Augustus'
son-in-law Marcellus erected awnings for the benefit
of the law-courts, and Caligula again set them up
during the exceptionally hot summer of AD 39. The
custom continued, for square holes for the wooden
posts of such awnings, which have been found incised
in the pavement of the Forum, date from the third
century AD or later still.

Pliny the elder (d. AD 79) had deplored the luxury.
'What a change,' he said, 'since the strenuous days of
Cato the Censor who proposed to pave the Forum
with small stones to keep idlers away!'[6] The poet
Horace would at least on one occasion (though surely
not always) have been glad if this had been done, for
it was just here, on the Sacred Way beside the Forum,
that he met his famous Bore, from whom he found it
impossible to escape.[7]

The Forum had always been full of such idlers, in
addition to people occupied with every sort of business. Its life, at the time when Cato the Censor was a
young man, is described by the Roman comic
dramatist Plautus (d. 184 BC) in his play *The Weevil*
or *Parasite (Curculio)*.

> I'll show you where to find all sorts of men,
> Or bad or good, or honest men or rascals.
> Whoe'er wants one to swear through thick and thin,
> I send him to law-courts – A lying boaster
> You'll find not far from Cloacina's altar.
> Your prodigal rich husbands you must look for
> At the Exchange. There too you'll find stale harlots,
> Ready for any bargain. Stewards of clubs
> Are ever at the fish-markets. Your rich,
> Your good men, at the bottom of the Forum.
> In th' middle, you shall have, near the canal,
> Mere braggarts, bold, loquacious – 'Bove the Lake,
> Malevolent and foul-mouthed fellows, such
> As boldly deal out slander without cause,
> Yet give sufficient matter unto others
> To form true accusations against them.
> At the Old Shops are those who lend out money,
> Or borrow it, on usury – Behind
> The temple of Castor, those you'll not trust easily.
> In Tuscan Street are such as sell themselves . . .[8]

Plautus' reference to the Old Shops recalls that, from
a very early date, the Forum had been lined with shops
and stalls. The Old Shops lay on the long south-
western side of the square. Facing away from the sun,
they had originally been let out mostly to provision
sellers. On the opposite side of the Forum were the
New Shops, which at first mainly belonged to fruiterers. But butchers were also prominent, and ac-
acording to an edifying legend it was from one of
their stalls that the father of the virtuous Verginia
seized a knife in order to kill his daughter and thereby
frustrate the lecherous attentions of Appius Claudius
(449 BC). The shrine of Cloacina, the spirit of the
Great Drain which passed nearby, was said, rather un-
romantically, to mark the spot. But in about the fourth
century BC the provision merchants on both sides of
the Forum were banished and replaced by the usurers
to whom Plautus refers – bankers, moneychangers,
silversmiths.

The official who substituted these dealers for the
humble food-sellers at the New Shops, and perhaps at
the Old Shops as well, seems to have been Gaius
Maenius, consul in 338 BC. His descendants constructed projecting balconies, known as Maeniana, on top
of the shops, New and Old, for the spectators of
entertainments in the Forum.[9] The Columna Maenia,
which was probably a pillar supporting one of these
galleries over the New Shops, served for a time as the
point where the last hour of the day was officially
determined by the setting of the sun. In 310 BC the
New Shops were adorned by shields captured from
Rome's Samnite enemies in central Italy. Subsequently
the stalls on both sides were incorporated into the
arcades of the great Basilicas, which will be described
in Chapter 7. At dramatic times, for example when the
bodies of Clodius and Caesar were cremated in the
Forum by violent multitudes, the shopkeepers fared
badly, since their benches and tables were forcibly
removed to feed the flames.

Around the Sacred Way, inscriptions have been
found referring to jewellers, goldsmiths and silversmiths, stone-cutters, bronze-chasers, florists, makers
of gold-embroidered dresses, pork-butchers, sellers of
honey and perfumes and ointments, chemists, lock-
smiths, cutlers, hairdressers, carpenters, fruiterers and
dealers in wind-instruments. The shops for jewellery
and metalwork were very fashionable, and particularly those of the experts in oriental pearls. But this
luxury market,[10] to which Nero and other emperors
added elegant colonnades, can nowadays barely be
reconstructed from a mass of shapeless rubble on the
Upper Sacred Way. In the same region there are also
remains of Domitian's bazaar for oriental spices
(*horrea piperataria*) – gutted by fires under Commodus
and Carinus, in AD 191 and 283. A neighbouring
huddle of small rooms seems to have been a wine-shop

Augustus wearing the veil of a priest:
from the Basilica Aemilia;
now in the Forum Museum.

A plan of the Forum after the reign of Augustus (d. AD 14).
By this time the crowded buildings, monuments
and statues were no longer a centre of everyday life but
rather a gigantic symbol of Roman Imperial glory.

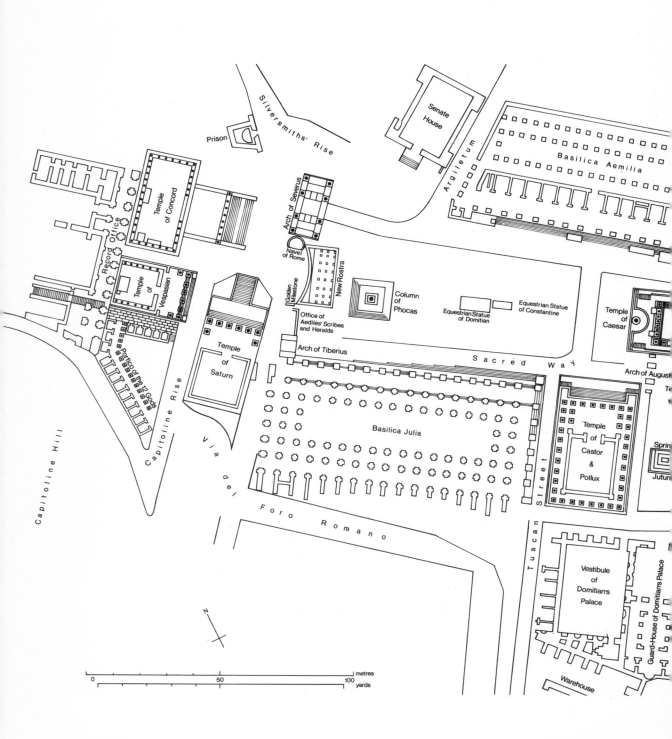

Capitoline Hill

Silversmiths' Rise

Prison

Record Office

Temple of Concord

Temple of Vespasian

Portico of the 12 Gods

Capitoline Rise

Via del

Foro Romano

Temple of Saturn

Arch of Severus

Navel of Rome

Golden Milestone

New Rostra

Office of Aediles' Scribes and Heralds

Arch of Tiberius

Column of Phocas

Equestrian Statue of Domitian

Senate House

Argiletum

Basilica Aemilia

Equestrian Statue of Constantine

Temple of Caesar

Sacred Way

Arch of August

Basilica Julia

Street

Tuscan

Temple of Castor & Pollux

Sprin

Jutur

Vestibule of Domitian's Palace

Guard-House of Domitian's Palace

Warehouse

N

0                    50                    100    metres
                                                  yards

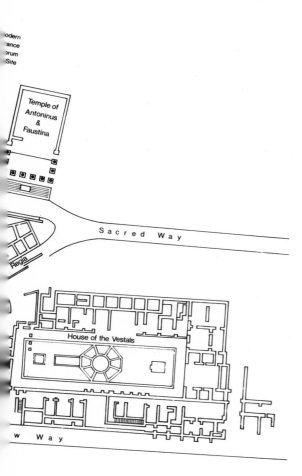

or cheap hotel, active in *c.* 80–50 BC. And nearer the main square itself, close to its north-eastern end, stands a small building in which sharp scholarly eyes have detected the built-in beds and narrow rooms of a brothel. Male prostitutes, however, as Plautus remarks, were to be found across the square in Tuscan Street, which also became famous for its scent-shops and in Horace's time possessed excellent booksellers, the Sosii.

Parallel to the Sacred Way was the New Way, and here, ensconced within the substructures of the Palatine, were many-storeyed buildings where shopkeepers lived above their shops in rooms lit by small windows surmounted by second floor apartments with windows grouped in threes. The street called the Argiletum, north-west of the Forum, housed bookshops, copyists, barbers and shoemakers; and it was in this region that some of the provision merchants who were moved out from the New Shops found their subsequent homes.

## FROM REPUBLIC TO EMPIRE

The masterful characters who successively governed Rome in its transition from Republic to Empire, Sulla, Caesar and Augustus, all left their decisive stamp on the physical appearance of the Forum. But it was under Augustus (d. AD 14) that the biggest changes came over its life. For now it became a sort of historical monument. His enormous replanning of Rome included a substantial overhaul of the Forum. But more important still, as the imperial regime got under way, was the fact that violent politics vanished from the scene. Although the law-courts, like the shops, were still crowded, they were no longer political battlegrounds. No one dared any more to make a rabble-rousing speech in the Forum; the only funeral oration likely to be heard was one glorifying the imperial regime. Moreover, Augustus' wild beast hunts in the Forum were the last of those dreadful entertainments to be seen there. Henceforward they were organized in more commodious spaces, and gladiatorial shows, too, were moved elsewhere. Besides, people could migrate to the rival splendours of the adjacent Imperial Fora, which successive emperors were building to supplement the Roman Forum (p. 43).

However, the old Forum still witnessed horrible happenings. It was here, in AD 69, that the elderly Galba was thrown sprawling from his travelling-chair

*Above:* Marble relief from the Forum, intricately carved
with the popular acanthus motif.
*Opposite:* Honorary columns in the Forum Romanum;
the statues crowning them have gone.

and killed. Anticipating a dreadful event, the crowds had hastily left the square, 'not to fly and disperse, but to possess themselves of the colonnades and elevated places of the Forum, as it might be to get places to see a spectacle.'[11]

And how numerous and indeed almost continuous, by that time, such vantage-points must have been! For a jostling mass of resplendent buildings had encroached on the Forum ever more closely. It was as though there were fifteen Westminster Abbeys each within a few yards of the next. And emperor after emperor continued to add new monuments in whatever space could be found, or to reconstruct the old ones in ever more grandiose form.

The claustrophobic atmosphere was intensified by a great mass of honorary arches and statues, and these, too, multiplied continually. By the end of antiquity Rome possessed as many as 3,785 bronze statues, and 22 great bronze equestrian statues, of emperors and generals. That was to say nothing of a host of images of other men, not to speak of gods. Nor does it include a vast number of effigies of marble which began to proliferate in imperial times (they came in useful as materials for a barricade on the Capitol during the Civil War of AD 69).

An enormous proportion of all this statuary stood in the immediate neighbourhood of the Forum. And many other statues towered over it from the steep pediments of the innumerable adjoining temples, 'crowned in Italian fashion', as Eugenie Strong described them, 'with tall upstanding figures which caught up the vertical movement of the columns and carried it upwards into space.'

This little, cramped area had ceased to be a living nucleus and had become a closely packed collection of revered museum pieces. Yet it was still the centre of the world; and the cities of the empire, whose inhabitants thronged to the place in all their polyglot diversity, were proud to erect inscriptions recording the presence of their offices and representatives. Tiberias in Israel is one such town whose announcement to this effect survives. A dedication by another city, after honouring the emperor Gordian III (238–44) in somewhat perfunctory fashion, heaps abundant praises on the dedicators' home-town: which is Tarsus, the birthplace of a Roman citizen of Jewish birth, St Paul, who is believed to have met his end in Rome.

## THE IMPACT OF THE FORUM

Finally Rome ceased to be a capital at all, since it was an economic parasite and seemed too remote from the danger-points of the empire. Constantine the Great built himself a new capital at Constantinople, and his son Constantius II, in the course of a long reign, made one visit and one only to the ancient mother-city (357). 'So then he entered Rome, the home of empire and of every virtue, and when he had come to the Rostra, the most renowned Forum of ancient dominion, he stood amazed; and on every side on which his eyes rested he was dazzled by the array of the marvellous sights.'[12] Soon afterwards the empire was permanently divided into separate eastern and western parts, and the western emperors preferred to live in north Italy rather than at Rome. But later still, after the last emperor of the west had been gone for a quarter of a century, the monk Fulgentius of Ruspe (AD 500) was as entranced by the ancient city as Constantius had been. 'Brethren,' he cried, 'how lovely must celestial Jerusalem be, if this is how earthly Rome glitters!'

Throughout the ages the Forum has continued to make an intense emotional impact on its visitors. For many centuries, as will be seen in Chapter 9, it was a place of ruins. But at the time when modern reconstructions were under way, people looked at the place with a heightened consciousness (Chapter 10). John Addington Symonds expressed something of the deep feeling and humility that comes upon an explorer of this amazing place today, just as it did in the nineteenth century.

Then, from the very soil of silent Rome,
You shall grow wise, and, walking, live again
The lives of buried peoples, and become
A child by right of that eternal home,
Cradle and grave of empires, on whose walls
The sun himself subdued to reverence falls.

Nevertheless, there is no denying that the lure of the Forum is also blended with strong elements of challenge. There are so many ruins, so imperfectly preserved. They are tightly compressed into so small a

space – though it will not seem as small when you have walked the whole length of the Forum and Sacred Way, mostly on Roman paving stones, and tried to see and decipher all that they have to show. A modern guide-book ventures to compare the site to a stone-mason's yard. How is one to attain an unimpeded view of what the Forum was, and what it meant?

It is possible, and indeed for a time enjoyable, to assume the elevated attitude of Byron, and enjoy the introxicating associations without attempting to identify particular buildings.

Who shall trace the void,
O'er the dim fragments cast a lunar light,
And say, 'here was, or is', when all is doubly night?

A great deal of history has been made in the Forum, and no special psychic gifts are needed to get the feel of it. But the place is so loaded with history that even the most highly developed psychic power in the world will not reveal more than a fraction of what is there. In order to get any substantial view of this panorama of the past, explanation is needed as well; and I have written this book in the hope of providing it.

As a first step, it is necessary to embark on the strange story of how the Forum came into existence.

*Below:* A model of ancient Rome, the Roman Forum running left to right through the centre.
*Opposite:* The Roman Forum looking east: in the foreground the Temple of Vespasian and to the right the Temple of Castor and Pollux and the Temple of Saturn.
*Overleaf left:* Between the vestibule of the Palace of Domitian and the warehouses of Agrippa and Germanicus.
*Overleaf right:* The New Way (Nova Via).

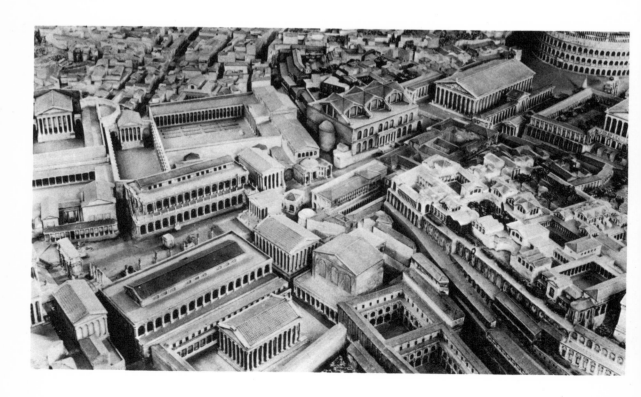

*Above:* The Forum site, bereft of its magnificent
veneer, displays its basic building materials. Here,
ruined columns rest against imperial brickwork
stripped of its marble or stucco covering.
*Left:* The Temple of Vesta.

ETRURIA

Via Triumphalis

R. Tiber

Via Flaminia

Field of Mars

Via Salaria

Via Nomentana

Servian Wall

Quirinal Hill

Viminal Hill

Via Tiburtina

Subura

Esquiline Hill

Capitoline Hill

Arx

Jupiter Capitolinus

Roman Forum

Fabrician Bridge

Tiber Island

Velian Slope

Janiculum Hill

Cestian Bridge

Forum Boarium

Palatine Hill

Via Aurelia

Aemilian Bridge

Sublician Bridge

Caelian Hill

Aventine Hill

Via Portuensis

Via Ostiensis

Via Appia

Via Latina

N

LATIUM

metres

0        500        1000

yards

# 2. The Beginnings of the Forum

## THE BEGINNINGS OF ROME

The Forum lies just over a mile from the left bank of the Tiber, at a point where the river passes beside the group of hills which were destined to become Rome. They were originally a good deal steeper than they are today. Fertile volcanic soil was not far off; nor was winter pasturage. Fifteen miles from the sea, the site was in a position to control the best cross-route of Italy and the principal line of communications along its western coast, where habitation was thicker than on the other side.

The skull of a single-tusked elephant that lived some two million years ago has been found in the alluvial sands of Rome, and a suburb has yielded the skull of a Neanderthal man more than thirty thousand years old. Other discoveries have included the flint and copper implements of people who lived in the place during the early second millennium before our era.

Historical Rome began to take shape in about 1000 BC, after the volcanic activities of the hills round about had ceased. The use of iron had begun, and groups of migrants, not only shepherds but farmers using light ploughs, gradually moved down north-westwards from the fringes of the Alban Mount and south-eastwards from the Sabine country, and built their huts upon the hills of Rome. These hills were a series of flat-topped spurs projecting from a low plateau towards the river; from north to south, the Quirinal, Viminal, Esquiline and Caelian. Newcomers also settled on an elevation between those spurs and the Tiber, the steep and almost isolated Palatine. The remaining two of the Seven Hills – on either side of the Palatine – were the precipitous Capitoline to its north-west and the Aventine to its south. These do not seem to have been settled at this early stage, though a

*Above:* Plan of the neighbourhood of Rome.
*Opposite:* Plan of the hills of Rome, showing the situation of the city between the territory of the Sabines and Latium, home of the Latins. Excavations show that settlers inhabiting the Palatine, Esquiline, and Caelian hills in the seventh century BC had forms of worship in common; tradition records that the Latins were the first to arrive, closely followed by the Sabines.

thatched hut on the former, which was still to be seen at the beginning of the Christian era, perhaps bears witness to the presence of an early observation post.[1]

A tradition recorded that the immigrants who came to the Palatine were Latins from the Alban Mount – their country, Latium, being the area that stretched south-east of the lower Tiber[2] – and that the settlers on the Quirinal and Esquiline were Sabines, people of mountain origin speaking a distinct but related Italic language. The Sabines were believed to have arrived on the site of Rome a little later than the Palatine Latins, who were therefore regarded as the city's true founders. These traditions are not implausible, though it is impossible to confirm them. The same may be said of Rome's legendary foundation date, 753 BC. But it may well be that future excavations will show a rival version favouring 814 BC to be closer to the mark.

Meanwhile archaeologists have already shown us that, early in the seventh century BC, villages on the Palatine (two), Esquiline (four) and Caelian (one) united with one another, even if this was only, at first, for purposes of common worship. By c. 650 the Palatine settlement or settlements had started taking an interest in the adjoining Tiber, where tracks converged on a cattle-market, the later Forum Boarium. Then, perhaps around c. 600, the northernmost spurs, the Quirinal and Viminal, joined the growing community. Not long afterwards a move was also made to incorporate the steep Capitoline hill, the future fortress and religious centre of Rome.

## WHEN THE FORUM WAS A CEMETERY

The Palatine, Capitoline and Esquiline hills adjoined and enclosed a marshy, moat-like valley which was the site of the future Roman Forum. A brook ran through it, and Virgil in his *Aeneid* looks back on those early days when the lowing of cattle was the only sound to be heard. There always remained relics of this remote swampy past. The most famous of them was the Pond of Curtius (Lacus Curtius), later adorned by altars and other structures; their bases still survive, roughly triangular in shape, and made of a building stone that was in use round 100 BC. Also on view, at the same spot, is the copy of a relief illustrating a famous story associated with the site. It shows Marcus Curtius propitiating the gods by leaping on horseback into a chasm that had opened there. This is one of several myths invented to explain the name, of which the true

*Above:* Detail from a painting by John Martin (1789–1854) of the legend of Marcus Curtius. Lord Kinross Collection.
*Right:* Relief of Marcus Curtius riding into the chasm to appease the anger of the god; found in 1553 near his pool (where a copy has been placed).
Museum of the Palazzo dei Conservatori.

significance had already been forgotten for ever.[3] But the depiction of waving reeds on the relief recalls that the site had really not been a chasm at all, but a bog. The poet, Ovid, who remarks that in his own day, at the time of Augustus, the place was quite dry, tells a story of how he was amazed to see a respectable woman walking down the adjacent New Way on bare feet. He was told that this was a traditional feature of the Festival of Vesta (whose shrine was nearby) dating back to the remote epoch when the region had been a swamp full of bulrushes and reeds.[4] A spring dedicated to the water-spirit Juturna (Chapter 4, pp. 87–90) was another of these survivals. Traces have also been found of very ancient, approximately rectangular wells, and even older ones that were round. These may go back to the time before there were any solid buildings in the Forum at all. If so, they were employed to provide water for cattle.

From time to time, ever since then, the Forum has received further reminders of its watery origin. In antiquity its ground-level was much lower than it is today, and floods were frequent and serious. Under Augustus alone, there were five inundations from the Tiber; Horace mentions a particularly damaging one.[5]

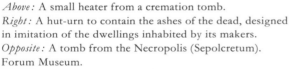

*Above:* A small heater from a cremation tomb.
*Right:* A hut-urn to contain the ashes of the dead, designed in imitation of the dwellings inhabited by its makers.
*Opposite:* A tomb from the Necropolis (Sepolcretum). Forum Museum.

Already before 700 BC the villagers on the Palatine and Esquiline hills employed parts of the Forum as cemeteries. They had also used their own hills for the same purpose; and the Quirinal community did the same. But space on the higher ground no doubt ran short. Moreover, at some stage or other, the idea grew up that the remains of the dead must not be laid within the limits of the human settlement. This veto is found in the Law of the Twelve Tables (451 BC).

The interments in the Forum are of two types, burial (inhumation) and cremation. When a body was buried, it was laid within an oblong grave or trench, either in a coffin made of a hollowed-out oak log or in a rough stone sarcophagus; or the trench was lined with stone panels. The cremation tombs, on the other hand, are small, deep, circular pits. Most of them contained a large globular jar with a stone slab as a lid. Within the jar stood an urn, often in the shape of a hut, containing the burnt ashes of the dead.

This sort of urn appears regularly in cremation tombs, but is exceptional in cases of burial; otherwise the objects deposited in the two types of grave are much the same. They include the remains of funeral offerings of food, as well as personal possessions of the dead – jars of 'biconical' shape (terminating at each end in a truncated cone), votive goblets, and two-handled cups. These vases are sometimes decorated with bosses and diamond-shaped designs. Ivory bracelets also appear, and glass pearls, and bronze pins ornamented with amber. Two small pins are made of silver, but gold is not found;[6] the Twelve Tables recorded an old Roman custom that no gold should be buried with the dead.

It used to be believed that inhumation was practised by the Sabines and cremation by the Latins. But the distinction should be stated in geographical rather than racial terms. Inhumations originated from the central Italian regions and cremations belonged to a more lowland chain of descent which extended from the Po valley down into south Etruria and then across the Tiber. Both rites are seen together on several of the Roman hills and within the Forum itself. In its archaic necropolis of forty graves (the Sepolcretum), which probably served both the Palatine and Esquiline communities, the two sorts of grave are even found cutting into one another. This site has now been closed up, but the finds can still be seen in the Forum Museum.

The conquests and expansions of the fabled Romulus and his first shadowy successors on the Roman throne are proudly recorded by Livy and others; but they are anachronistic myth. Rome of the eighth and seventh centuries BC was not such an impressive power. All the same, its horizons were widening. For excavations indicate that by 650 BC close relations had been established with Falerii (Città Castellana), a town lying twenty-eight miles northwards on the other side of the Tiber. Like Rome, Falerii was a place of mixed culture, for it was on the border between the great, rising Etruscan cities (see pp. 37–39) and the less advanced Sabines and Latins. Rome, though smaller, was the same sort of frontier town as Falerii.

In order to facilitate external contacts, the Romans built their first wooden bridge across the river, the Pons Sublicius. They also established a fort at Ostia beside the river mouth. Both acts were later attributed to the half-legendary king Ancus Marcius, and the early dates which this implies (640–616 BC) are not impossible. Archaeology, it is true, has so far been unable to prove them; but it is able to add that there were close links, indeed something like cultural integration, with the Alban Mount fifteen miles to the south.

## THE FORUM
## BECOMES THE MAIN SQUARE

When Rome was reaching this increased, though still humble degree of importance, its people began to appreciate that the Forum, almost encircled by the hills and their habitations, showed possibilities far exceeding those of a mere marshy burial place. And so a beginning was now made with its drainage.

Excavation of a section of the Forum, equidistant from the Palatine and Esquiline, has disclosed not only a geographical extension of the necropolis but evidence of the first permanent occupation of the area, dating back, apparently, to c. 670–660 BC. Here are the remnants of about a dozen huts. The marks of their foundations can be seen, and beaten earth floors, and holes in the ground to lodge upright posts – no doubt branches of trees bent inwards and tied together at the top. These remains, resembling hut circles on Dartmoor, are very like others of somewhat earlier date that have been found on the neighbouring Palatine. What evidently happened was that overcrowding in the hill villages had caused some of their inhabitants

to move down the slopes and build in the area that had previously served as their cemetery.

These traces on the ground, supplemented by the hut-shaped designs of the cremation urns found in the tombs, indicate that the dwellings were clay-daubed, roughly oval structures of interwoven straw and twigs, possessing steep, thatched roofs with overhanging edges. The door was square or rounded and secured by a cross bar, and it was sometimes approached through a crude pillared porch.

For the next half century or so, the Forum continued to comprise not only huts but new tombs as well. In c. 620 the first dwellings seem to have been destroyed by floods. Drainage of a more systematic kind was undertaken, and henceforward the huts extended over a wider area, including the lowest-lying parts of the Forum. Burials and cremations, on the other hand, dwindled and soon came to an end.

By c. 575 the Forum was being transformed into a pebble-floored market place.[7] It was approached by simple streets (pp. 44–49) and adjoined by the Old Shops (SW) and by stuccoed mud-brick houses with clay-tiled roofs and foundations made of small stones. Then, after c. 550, there were no houses left beside the main square at all. For the town of Rome was coming into existence. The Forum was its public centre, and private habitations had to move elsewhere.

The population now included not only farmers and shepherds but merchants and craftsmen as well. Already before 600 BC, a burial on the Esquiline showed the remains of armour and a chariot; and over the intervening decades signs of wealth and importance had increased. Finds from the second quarter of the sixth century include pieces of terracotta which were intended for the external decoration of shrines and other buildings. They display reliefs of religious and mythological scenes: Gorgons' heads, Minotaurs, galloping horsemen, lionesses, panthers: and the designs become more and more sophisticated.

Latin neighbours may have contributed to this art, but its real inspiration comes from the Etruscans. Some centuries earlier these people, who called themselves the 'Rasenna', had established twelve independent city-states in what is now southern Tuscany and northern Lazio, covering a territory of two hundred miles from the River Arno to the Tiber and Apennines. Whatever the truth of the tradition that they, or some of them, had come from the east, their art looked eastern because it was a provincial adaptation

Terracotta plaque showing a Minotaur flanked by two
animals, possibly lioness and panther, early sixth
century BC; found on the site of the later Arch of Augustus,
now in the Forum Museum.

Frieze on a terracotta basin of the sixth century BC probably showing ritual dancing with bulls; found on the Sacred Way and now in the Forum Museum.

of Greek art, a very imaginative and energetic adaptation, effected at a time when the Greeks were subject to orientalizing trends. And in the seventh century BC Etruria supplemented these influences by its own direct contacts with the Anatolians and Assyrians and above all with the Phoenicians from the coast of the Levant. These Phoenicians had their own harbour facilities at Etruscan ports – and probably at Rome as well.

Before 650, Tarquinii, forty miles north-west of Rome, had taken over the pre-eminence from more northerly Etruscan cities, largely owing to its vigorous bronze industry. By the next century, however, the dominant role had moved still further south to towns only a very short distance from the Tiber, Caere (Cerveteri) and then from *c.* 550 Veii, a mere eight miles from Rome. Roman tradition maintained that two of its own last three monarchs, each called Tarquinius – Priscus (616–578) and his son Superbus (534–510) – had both been Etruscans. How many Etruscan rulers there really were at Rome is unknown, but what is certain is that during the greater part of the sixth century BC, and perhaps also for a generation or two before and after, Rome was controlled for most of the time by an Etruscan dynasty or dynasties.

They were the men who within half a dozen decades, supported by an army of heavy-armed infantry, transformed the place into a city and made the Forum its town-centre. The temple they built on the Capitoline Hill, dedicated to the supreme god whom the Romans called Jupiter, competed in size with almost any shrine throughout the Greek world, and remained the largest in Rome for half a millennium to come. Not surprisingly, the terracotta reliefs found in the Forum are particularly reminiscent of neighbouring Caere and Veii. Pottery and metal-work from the same cities made their appearance as well, and the foundations and roof-tiles of the Forum's short-lived houses were likewise Etruscan in character.

The name of a road leading to the bridge, Tuscan Street (p. 49), may reflect the presence of Etruscan workmen, brought to build the Capitoline temple. Or the quarter may have been occupied by Etruscan shopkeepers, who thus remained within easy reach of Veii, since that city, as air photographs have shown, was linked to Rome by a very early road or path. Livy and others have listed institutions which the Romans owed to Etruria. Their architecture, art, engineering and ritual all possessed extensive debts of this nature. And although the Etruscan language has yielded only relatively few of its secrets, a number of its words, including proper names, gained new life because they passed into the Latin tongue.

Among the remains brought to light in the Forum are many Etruscan imitations of Greek pots. They recall the story that Tarquinius Priscus had originally been a Greek from Corinth, which during this period was at the height of its power as a maritime trading community. Whether the account of Priscus' Greek origin was in itself true or not, the Forum, like other parts of Rome, has yielded numerous discoveries of vases that have come from Corinth and Athens – which succeeded Corinth in the maritime supremacy – as well as from other Greek ports. These finds bear witness to early Rome's direct contacts with Greece.

Other vases discovered in the Forum are imitations of Corinthian ware, the products of Greek towns of south Italy. With these places Rome had already established a long-standing connection, reflected in Virgil's legend supposing that a Greek king, Evander, had ruled over the Palatine before the mythical founder Romulus himself. The manufactures of Greek south Italy were often brought up by land, via Satricum (Conca) thirty miles south-east of Rome. They could also be conveyed by sea as far as the Tiber mouth, from which they were transferred in barges up to the quays of Rome itself. The first foreign god to receive a cult at Rome was of Greek origin. He was Hercules, the same as the Greek Heracles, and his open-air altar on the river-bank beside the old cattle-market was the scene of rites conducted in the Greek fashion, with the worshippers' heads uncovered (Chapter 4, p. 76).

But the Etruscans lived much nearer at hand than the Greeks, and it was they who exercised the most direct and decisive influence on Rome. They had acquired from their eastern contacts a knowledge of drainage, which they developed in highly expert fashion, as the

cisterns, shafts and tunnels round Veii still show. Rome owed one of the Tarquins its Great Drain, the Cloaca Maxima.[8] Incorporating a stream that had originally been the border between the Roman settlement and the Quirinal (at the time when the latter was still outside the city), the drain collected various brooks which ran through the valleys between the hills; and then it passed through the eastern end of the Forum before reaching the Tiber. There the arched vaults of its debouchment into the river can still be seen. The curved tops of the arches themselves are unlikely to be older than the second century BC, but the side walls that support them include far more ancient materials.

But for a long time the drain was still an open ditch or canal. Even as late as 168 (or 159) BC the Greek philosopher Crates of Mallus had the misfortune to fall into a section of this trench, at a point beside the Palatine. He broke a leg, and, obliged to stay on in the

*Above:* Reconstruction of the Shrine of Venus Cloacina.
*Left:* The Cloaca Maxima; its outlet into the Tiber.
*Below:* The Shrine of Venus Cloacina on a silver coin of Lucius Mussidius Longus, *c.* 42 BC.

*Below :* The Forum of Julius Caesar, first of the Imperial Fora.
*Opposite :* The Temple of Venus Genetrix in the Forum of Julius Caesar.

city, proceeded to give lectures which greatly stimulated Roman interest in scholarship.[9]

The importance of the drain had been recognized at an early date by the worship of its godhead or spirit or power, Cloacina. Later identified (strangely) as a manifestation of Venus, she was given a shrine in the Forum, where parts of a round travertine[10] substructure and marble rim survive.

This Forum itself, the main 'square', was an open oblong area measuring about 300 feet by 200. Its original shape followed the points of the compass, with the long sides and their monuments facing due north and south, according to deliberate religious intention. But when Sulla and Caesar reconstructed the area towards the end of the Republic, this cardinal orientation was shifted so that the long sides of the Forum, as

*Above:* Marble relief with fantastic animals and acanthus
spirals; originally decorating the Sacred Way, now
exhibited on a medieval structure in the Basilica Aemilia.
*Opposite:* Plan of the Imperial Fora built beside
the Roman Forum.

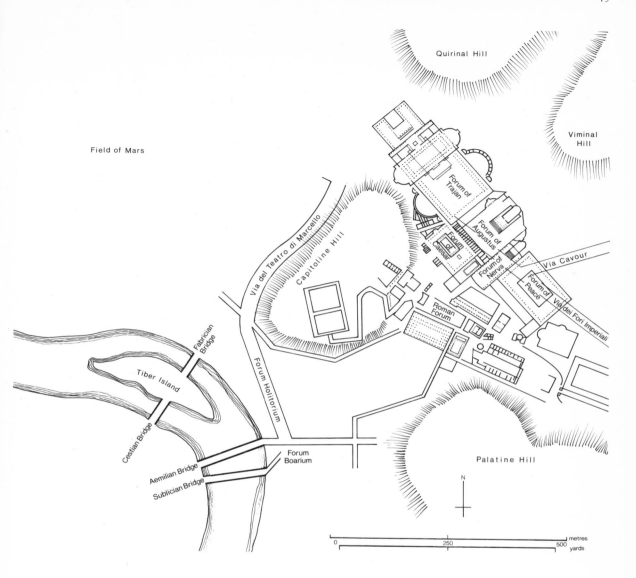

we see it, face approximately the north-east and south-west.

The principal rectangular meeting-place of an Italian town was normally called its Forum, though usually these piazzas lay in the geographical centres of their towns, which the Roman Forum did not. The ancients thought the word 'Forum' came from *ferre*, 'to bring' – the place where people brought things for purposes of trade – but probably it is instead connected with *foras*, meaning 'outside', because the Forum was originally outside the boundaries of the inhabited hill-villages.

Later, in imperial times, this historic area was called

the 'Roman' or 'Great' Forum, to distinguish it from the adjoining and supplementary Imperial Fora, which were vast precincts built by Caesar, Augustus, Vespasian, Nerva and Trajan on the north-east flank of the old main square. But even in early ages there had already been other, separate Fora at Rome, for the sale of cattle, pigs, fish and vegetables. However, the true Forum of the city of Rome was always the Forum Romanum, the subject of the present book. It was regarded as comprising the buildings round the main rectangle together with a supplementary piece of ground (Forum Adjectum) extending to the south-east as far as the Arch of Titus.

## ALL ROADS LEAD TO THE FORUM

Before the villages united, tracks had tended to converge at the cattle market on the river. But once the communities merged, all roads radiated instead to and from the Forum Romanum – as reference to the map below will show.

primitive days had acted as a boundary between the hills (p. 39), and was in due course canalized and covered. This part of the thoroughfare, unlike the smarter Low section beside the Forum, became rather disreputable. Plautus comments unfavourably on the seedy sort of people who lingered by the canal, and their Latin name, *canalicolae*, is the origin of the French

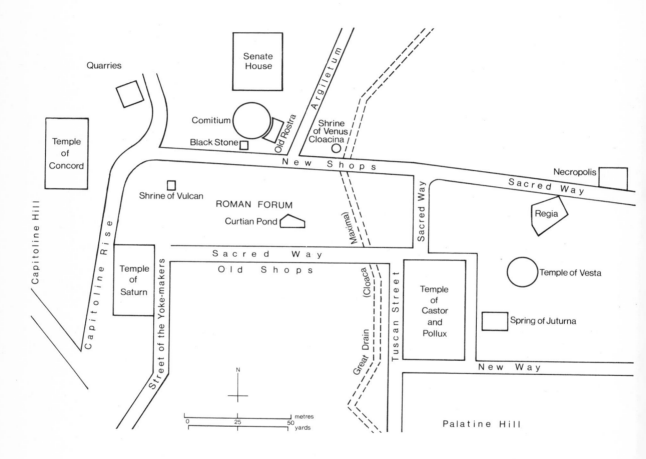

(1) The earliest of these thoroughfares was the Via Sacra or Sacred Way. It left the north-eastern end of the Forum to pass up the Velia, a low saddle linking the Palatine and Esquiline hills. Later on, an extension of the street down on the side away from the Forum (to a point near the Colosseum) was also regarded as part of the Sacred Way, and so, at the other end, was its continuation round the SE and SW edges of the Forum itself. The main part of the Way, between these two extensions, was regarded as divided into three very short sections, Top, Middle and Low. The Middle section followed the course of an old stream which in

*canaille*. However, great shrines were very close by, and the name 'Sacred' may be owed to their presence, unless, as some Romans believed, it originated from the religious processions for which the street was habitually used.

Several early street levels of the Sacred Way, one above the other, have partially survived, disclosing a thick and solid surface of stones, gravel and pebbles.

The Sacred Way leading up the Velian Slope to the Arch of Titus.

*Above:* Imaginative reconstruction of the Sacred Way rising from the Basilica Nova of Maxentius and Constantine.
*Opposite:* The Via Nova or New Way, its stately arches spanning a strangely narrow artery to the heart of the ancient world.

The earliest of these road-beds seems to go back to *c.* 575 BC, the epoch when the Forum first came into existence. By the fifth century BC, part of the road was supported by a massive substructure to protect it against rain. Yet paved streets probably did not exist for another three hundred years. Much later still, Nero equipped the Sacred Way with splendid colonnades leading up to the vestibule of his palace (the Golden House, Appendix 2).

(2) The second oldest street in Rome, known as the Via Nova or New Way, ran parallel to the Sacred Way. The New Way provided a second south-eastern egress from the Forum, this time running under the shadow of the Palatine, as far as the gate which gave admission to that hill.[11] Although called 'New', the road dates back at least as far as the venerable monarchic period of Rome; rather as New College is one of the oldest establishments in Oxford.

Within the city no street except these two most ancient ones bore the name of 'Via', which, centuries later, also came to be applied to the great roads leading out of Rome to other parts of Italy.

(3) Other streets in the city were mostly known as 'Vici', and three of them led south-west, in each case

The underground passage or Cryptoporticus built by
Nero in the Palatine Hill, leading to the Forum.

towards the vicinity of the riverside cattle-market. Vicus Tuscus or Tuscan Street, which (as indicated earlier) owed its name to an Etruscan connection, started from the Forum at the same SE corner as the New Way but ran at right angles to it, leading down to the earliest Tiber bridge, the Pons Sublicius. Under the surviving portions of the lava surface of Tuscan Street, small irregular blocks belonging to an older pavement have come to light. Later the name was changed to Vicus Turarius or Street of the Spice-Sellers, whose shops were concentrated here. At the beginning of the street, beside the Forum, there was a very low-grade slave traffic, as well as the male prostitution mentioned by Plautus.

(4) From the south-western corner of the Forum the Vicus Jugarius or Street of the Yoke-Makers passed along the foot of the Capitoline and reached the Tiber opposite an island which had provided a stepping-stone for early crossings.

(5) A third thoroughfare leaving the Forum in this same direction was the Clivus Victoriae or Victory Rise,[12] where Cicero and the glamorous Clodia (whom he hated) both had their residences. Starting just beyond Tuscan Street, this reached the cattle-market by skirting round the steep western sides of the Palatine. When the substructures of imperial palaces on that hill blocked the exit of Victory Rise from the Forum, a slanting flight of steps under a covered tunnel was provided as a replacement for this short initial portion of the way.[13]

(6) The steep street leading upwards from the north-western end of the Forum to the Capitoline heights was the Clivus Capitolinus or Capitoline Rise. Discoveries of its pavement thirty years ago showed that in spite of the high gradient it ran straight and cut the ridge obliquely, with the support of a viaduct-like substructure, before turning sharply right to reach the Temple of Jupiter on the summit. Although this paving has now been raised in some places, and for one stretch it is incorporated in a modern street (the Via del Foro Romano), the ancient blocks are still to be seen. They are mostly of imperial date (i.e. after 31 BC), but underneath lies an earlier surface attributed to 174 BC, consisting of hard rough lava slabs. Like the Sacred Way, of which it formed the continuation for Triumphal processions, the Capitoline Rise was flanked by a serried mass of columns and statues, as well as by the porticoes which served contestants in the Civil War of AD 69 as a vantage-point from which they could bombard enemies below with blocks of stone and tiles.

(7) The later Clivus Argentarius or Silversmiths' Rise left the Forum at its north-eastern corner and ran up the valley between the Capitoline and Quirinal hills, where stone quarries *(lautumiae)* had originally been situated. Its pavement is visible today (behind the adjacent Forum of Caesar, where the Via di Marforio used to be). The name 'Argentarius' is only known from early medieval times, but was probably a good deal earlier. It may have been taken from a neighbouring Basilica Argentaria, which cannot now be located but no doubt stood on the Rise. Under some name or other, this street must have been ancient, for it was Rome's main link with the Campus Martius or Field of Mars, the low-lying area in the bend of the Tiber, which was gradually filled up with monuments and gardens but remained outside the city walls until the third century AD.

(8) Finally, still on the north-east side of the Forum, the street known as the Argiletum led between the Esquiline and Viminal hills up a valley known as the Subura, a noisy trading quarter which gained fame as the birth-place of Julius Caesar. The Romans fancifully derived Argiletum from the mythical Argus, a guest of King Evander detected in treachery,[14] but probably the word comes from *argilla*, clay, referring to local clay-pits and a quarter occupied by potters.

No less than eight roads, then, linked the Forum with the outside world. They were venerable and famous. But they were always very narrow, and even schemes of urbanization, such as Nero's attempt to improve the squalid residential accommodation of the city, did little or nothing to broaden them, though he furnished the Sacred Way with handsome lateral arcades. As Professor Jerome Carcopino writes about the Sacred and New Ways, 'the insignificance of these two thoroughfares remains a perpetual surprise'. And the others, too, were remarkably small. The Street of the Yoke-Makers measured only sixteen and a half feet across, and Tuscan Street only thirteen and a half.

## THE BLACK STONE

The Romans told a highly improving patriotic tale of a national rising in 510 BC which ejected Tarquinius Superbus and abolished the Etruscan monarchy, replacing it by the historic Republic led by two annually elected consuls. Modern criticism has cast a sceptical eye on every detail of this dramatic transformation scene. However, it can at least still be said with confidence that by 500, or perhaps 450, Rome had ceased to be under the Etruscans and was no longer a monarchy but a Republic controlled by people of native origin. Moreover, like Falerii and other towns which had likewise been temporarily subjected to the Etruscans, Rome emerged speaking its own Indo-European tongue: in this case Latin, destined for literary glory.

The first known Latin inscription was found at the Latin town of Praeneste (Palestrina), twenty-three miles from Rome; and another has come to light on Rome's Quirinal Hill. The latter document is probably of c. 525 BC. The years immediately following that date have produced a further important inscription which was discovered at a point on the very edge of the Forum itself. This mysterious site, lying about five feet below the later surface, is known as the Lapis

The Black Stone (Lapis Niger), enigmatic square monument of black marble slabs, alleged by ancient authors to be an especially sacred place.

Niger, Black Stone, because it is roofed by a square pavement of six strips of black marble, probably from Greece. The pavement was originally enclosed by a three-foot balustrade of narrow white marble slabs. The inscription was found underneath the pavement along with other objects, including a truncated cone of yellowish volcanic stone. There are also two small quadrangular structures, one of which is adjoined by two broad stone pedestals. Nearby was a votive deposit (i.e. in fulfilment of a vow), or perhaps it was merely a refuse heap. It disclosed fragments of terracotta reliefs.

Ancient authors write of this Black Stone, and indicate that the paving was placed there to mark a sacred place.[15] It is variously described as the tomb of Hostus, father of Tullus Hostilius the semi-mythical third King of Rome (672–640 BC), or the tomb of the first king Romulus himself, or of the shepherd Faustulus who was said to have discovered the infant Romulus and Remus and brought them up. No actual grave, however, has so far been found, and there are no signs of a funeral monument, so that some scholars have preferred to accept an alternative view that the area was never a tomb at all but became thought of as sacred because a man had been killed there by lightning. But the literary record indicates that the two pedestals were for statues of lions, such as the Etruscans placed in front of important graves; and so the theory of a tomb remains valid. Thirteen stone bases, of comparable form and date, have now been discovered at Lavinium, which was twelve miles south of Rome and allegedly its parent city.[16] But they, too, are difficult to interpret. As for the Roman monument, every one of its numerous enigmatic aspects has produced what Professor Pietro Romanelli calls 'heated discussions'.

The inscription found beneath the black marble is written on a rectangular piece of stone, in lines proceeding alternately from left to right and right to left. The original is now in the Forum Museum,[17] but a replica has been set up at the place where the discovery was made. The inscription, written in very early Latin, is so seriously damaged that not a single line is complete. However, it clearly represents a piece of ritual law, and the opening words are translatable as a warning that the man who damages, defiles or violates the spot will be cursed. One reconstruction of the text interprets it as referring to the misfortune which could be caused if two yoked draught cattle should happen, while passing by, to drop excrement simultaneously. The coincidence would constitute a perilous evil omen.

Beneath the Black Stone;
a copy of the mysterious inscription, of which
the original is in the Forum Museum.

The inscription twice refers to a *rex*, as well as mentioning the *kalator* who was his servant and attendant. This allusion to a 'king' would not in itself prove that the inscription belonged to the regal age (ending in the late sixth or mid-fifth century BC) rather than the subsequent Republic, because in Republican times there still survived an official known as *rex* – the *rex sacrorum*, who took over certain religious functions from the monarchs (p. 72). But the uppermost stratum of soil *beneath* the surviving foundations contains no material later than the sixth century BC. It seems likely, therefore, that this inscription does belong to the regal period, and that the word *rex* refers to one of the last of these prehistoric monarchs, reigning not very long after the original inauguration of the Forum as a public place (*c.* 575). This conclusion likewise fits the form of the Latin characters employed, which somewhat resemble letters found in inscriptions of similar date from Lavinium and Falerii. There are also analogies with Greek letters employed in southern Italy, and with the writing of the Etruscans to whom Rome, though developing its own Italic language, was probably indebted for its alphabet.

The structures beneath the Black Stone are all truncated at the top, evidently by some deliberate act. The black pavement itself was apparently moved or reconstructed on at least one occasion, and perhaps more. For its level is much above that of the ancient relics below, and the most recent objects found in the adjacent votive deposit or rubbish dump are as late as the first century BC or AD. That is to say, the black marble stones do not seem to have been laid in their present positions until then. Perhaps Caesar or Augustus, in the course of reconstruction work, had to disturb these ancient monuments. In that case, whichever of them was responsible for doing so will have felt obliged to undertake a ritual sealing of the site, in the hope of expiating the violation of these ancient, venerable and, even at that time, incomprehensible relics.

Second side of the inscription beneath the Black Stone (see also p. 51). This replica stands on the site in place of the original which is in the Forum Museum.

# Part 2

# The Buildings of the Forum

# 3. The Most Sacred Precinct

## THE TEMPLE OF VESTA

The shrine which by its shape and associations most nearly recalls those distant days is the small round Temple of Vesta. We can admire today, reconstructed from the ruins in 1930, a considerable and elegant portion of the later external facings of the temple (*c.* AD 200), their original white marble supplemented by modern travertine. A portion of two concentric rows of fluted columns is also to be seen, with three still standing in each circuit. The inner row are engaged in the wall of the shrine, and the outer row, upon high square plinths, stand out from it so as to leave a narrow portico round the whole temple. The columns display the decorative acanthus leaves of the Corinthian Order, which the Romans generally preferred to the simpler Doric and Ionic. Above them is the traditional horizontal crown (entablature) of classical architecture, with its three superimposed parts of lintel (architrave), frieze and cornice. The frieze is decorated with reliefs representing sacrificial implements.

The outer columns were linked together by bronze gratings. The stone base of the temple, now visible, was masked in ancient times by four steps all round the circumference. The roof, which has now gone, consisted of a circular dome with a central opening surmounted by a sort of bronze shield which protected the interior from wind and rain. Outside the little building on either side were statues of gods.

These are some of the features that can be deduced from representations on coins. The temple, or something like it, is also shown on a relief in the Uffizi Gallery at Florence. But this shows column-capitals with the characteristic spirals of the Ionic Order, not the Corinthian that are actually to be seen on the building itself. Perhaps, then, the relief records the temple

*Above:* The Temple of Vesta depicted on a gold coin of Vespasian (AD 69–79). The central statue of the goddess Vesta stood, in fact, in a separate shrine outside the House of the Vestals.

*Opposite:* The partly-restored remains of the Temple of Vesta, the most sacred building in Rome.

Marble relief of a Temple of Vesta with Ionic capitals,
possibly Augustus' Temple of Vesta on the Palatine Hill.
Uffizi Gallery, Florence.

in an earlier form than the structure we see today. It is also possible, however, that the circular shrine represented on the relief is not this Temple of Vesta at all but a similar though not identical copy built on the Palatine Hill by Augustus.

Although the exterior of the temple beside the Forum, as we see it, is duly decked out with the classical architectural motifs, its circular shape directly and by unbroken continuity goes back to the primitive huts depicted in the hut-urns used for prehistoric cremations (Chapter 2, p. 34). In its beginnings Vesta's temple had been one of these roundish or oval huts, or something very like it.[1] As Ovid reported,

> That fabric which now wears a golden awe
> was then with osiers weaved and thatched with straw.[2]

The location of the door of the shrine, which stands at the cardinal point of the east, is another feature recalling its antique origins. The shrine was burnt down on a number of occasions[3] (including the Great Fire under Nero, which stopped short of the Forum itself but reached this point), but each time the subsequent reconstruction retained the ancient shape and eastern direction.

The reason why the temple proved so inflammable was because it was devoted to the cult of the sacred fire. The fire symbolized the perpetuity of the Roman state, and must never be allowed to go out. Its extinction was taken as a fearful prodigy announcing the destruction of the nation, for a cold hearth meant an uninhabited house. The cult was paralleled in the private worship of all devout Roman families: a fire was kept alight on every domestic hearth, and after the first and chief course of the mid-day meal, when silence had been ordered, a portion of the food was thrown from a sacrificial dish into the flame.

Inside the temple there is nothing to be seen today except a circular platform covered by two layers of stone blocks and pierced by a pit of irregular rectangular shape, originally twenty-six feet deep, which was probably used to store the ashes and other refuse from the rites. But these remains do not date back to the earliest times, and the original shrine has completely gone. However, a votive deposit within its area contained material going back as far as *c.* 575–550 BC. This includes Greek and Etruscan pottery, pins and tiles. Some of the pots are evidently not funerary but domestic in character – intended to fit into kitchen ovens, perhaps in the neighbouring House of the Vestals, which will be described in the next section.

Yet even these early finds may not represent anything like the first days of the temple. The Romans attributed the shrine, like many other antique religious institutions, to the second of their kings, Numa Pompilius, who was believed to have reigned from 715 to 672 BC. He may never have existed; but the attribution of the cult to this august figure means that it was known to be of very ancient origin.

At an even earlier date still, it appears, the village on the adjoining Palatine Hill had possessed a fire cult of its own;[4] and the present temple may well have been an offshoot of this. It is understandable that the cult should have been moved down the hill. For as the Palatine village had grown larger and more tightly packed, there seemed good reason to transfer this communal fire, which was no doubt larger than those of individual houses, away from the inhabited zone in order to lessen the danger of conflagration. The necessity of such a precaution was underlined by the fact that even in historical times the building, in spite

Imaginative reconstruction of the Temple of Vesta, its doors open for worshippers and the smoke of the undying flame issuing from the chimney.

of all its stone construction and careful maintenance, went up in flames so often.

The Temple of Vesta was unique in many respects. For one thing there was the paradox that it was not a temple in the technical Roman sense at all, since it did not, like the others, stand upon ground formally set apart for the use of the gods after proper consultation of the omens. And yet the building remained quite exceptionally and awesomely sacred. Prayers and sacrifices were often concluded with the name of this deity.[5] 'Far more than any other cult,' as W. Warde-Fowler said, 'that of Vesta represents the reality and continuity of Roman religious feeling.'

Visits to this most holy of places could be terrifying. When Nero planned to leave Rome for an eastern tour, 'he proceeded to the Capitol for consultation about his journey. After worshipping the Capitoline gods, he entered the shrine of Vesta. But there all his limbs suddenly began to tremble. The goddess frightened

The Temple of Vesta on a silver coin of Nero.

him. Or perhaps he was always frightened, remembering his crimes. At all events, he abandoned his journey.'[6]

The temple was also in demand as a sanctuary, or at least a place of refuge. It retained its potency in men's minds. When cults of the individual pagan deities began to fail during the third century of our era, and people increasingly thought of these Olympians as aspects and manifestations of a single pagan divinity, Vesta defied the process of decline. Her temple does not vanish from the coins, and inscriptions continue to show many dedications in her name – extending well beyond AD 300, and even beyond Constantine's subse-

quent official conversion of the Empire to Christianity.

For this cult of the Fire, paralleled in the fire-worship of the empire's Persian neighbours, evoked a response in Romans of those days. They were imbued with a feeling that their monotheistically conceived god was the Sun; and the light of the Sun and of Vesta's fire appeared to be the same. Above all, in the grim days of the later empire when external and internal menaces were pressing, the pagan worshippers, now on the defensive, concentrated on the powers that protected Rome: and Vesta was the city's age-long, everlasting guardian.

Coins that depict Roman temples maintain certain artificial conventions in their methods of representing them. Thus numismatic pictures of the temple of Vesta are misleading because they often display a statue of the goddess, either seated or standing, in the centre of the building. In fact, however, one of the peculiarities of this shrine was that it possessed no such statue. The poet Ovid had at first believed there was one, he says, but later he discovered that this had been a mistake.[7]

Instead there was an image of Vesta in a little chapel outside the building, a few steps away. The chapel has recently been reconstructed from remains that are partly of the second century AD. But this sort of personification of the goddess does not go back to the

remotest past. The early Romans had not been so ready as the Greeks to personify the divine forces that they worshipped. A Roman found it far easier to venerate the powers or spirits which lurked in objects and places and to regard them as impersonal. Such a power or *numen* was Vesta, whom Ovid declares to be 'nothing but a living flame'.

However, even in quite early times the Romans, under the influence of Greek culture, began gradually to go through the motions of identifying their own divinities with the more humanized deities of the Greeks, thus personalizing them and investing them with Greek mythologies and genealogies. And in spite of the essentially non-human character of Vesta, it was easy to identify her with the Greek hearth-goddess Hestia, especially as the two names were etymologically connected. And so in due course she was given effigies and endowed with a family tree of divine relatives. Yet her cult always remained fundamentally impersonal, as it had been in the beginning.

Inside the shrine a space or niche, probably screened off by tapestries, contained the Roman Holy of Holies, the *penus* of Vesta. *Penus* means store or provision of food. Originally, we are told, it signified actual stored food and drink, but then it came to mean the receptacle in which this was kept. The *penus* of a private home contained its food supplies. No one but children was

*Opposite left:* Gold coin of AD 214, the bicentenary year of the death and deification of Augustus, showing Caracalla sacrificing before the Temple of Vesta.
*Left:* The Temple of Vesta flanked by a voting tablet inscribed AC (*absolvo, condemno*) to the right, and a voting urn to the left, on a silver coin of Quintus Cassius, *c.* 57 BC.
*Above:* Brass coin showing the Temple of Vesta, issued by Tiberius (AD 14–37) in honour of the deified Augustus.

supposed to touch them there, to make sure that the purity of the place should not be defiled by impure hands. In the same way the Storehouse of Vesta stood for the grain-store of the state – it was a sanctified guarantee that the people would survive.

The guardians of the *penus*, whether in a private home or in this symbolic national Storehouse, were the Penates, who also had a temple of their own somewhere on the Velian slope, not far away. Their name probably owes its plural form to the variety of the provisions they had to guard. Every family larder had its Penates, and in their capacity as divine powers guarding the nation's store in the Temple of Vesta

they were known as *di penates publici*. They and Vesta
shared an antique place of worship at Rome's alleged
mother city, Lavinium. The Romans did not know
where the cult of the Penates had come from, but
identified them with gods of the Aegean island of
Samothrace, and declared that Aeneas, the mythical
forerunner of Romulus, had brought them from there
on his migration from the ruins of burning Troy.[8]

They were habitually associated with the Lares, who
may originally have been powers guarding farms. But
then, like the Penates, they were imported to the city
in the capacity of national as well as household gods.
And they too were given a shrine, at the summit of
the Sacred Way.

Each year, the new crop of grain became more and
more sacred as harvest-time approached, reaching the
climax of its sanctity when the Festival of Vesta was
celebrated in early June. At all other seasons the Storehouse was kept shut, but on 7 June it was thrown open
to all married women, and for seven days they crowded
into it barefoot. Then it was closed again. But first it
had been carefully purified. The refuse was thrown
into the Tiber or removed elsewhere, probably after
storage in the deep pit that has been found beneath the
shrine. This hole must have contained some pretty
gruesome material, such as the ashes of the calves
torn by attendants of the Chief Vestal from the corpses
of thirty-one pregnant cows slaughtered and cremated
on 15 April every year. Six days later the ashes, mixed
with blood, were poured onto heaps of burning straw
over which people jumped in a weird ceremony of
purification.

When these performances had all taken place, the
Storehouse was at last ready to receive the new grain:
though it could still only be stored and eaten after
elaborate ritual precautions. For the traditions from
remote antiquity which centred upon the Storehouse
of Vesta were very numerous. It housed, for example,
a jar containing the blood from the head of a race-
horse which was decapitated and sacrificed to Mars
every October.[9]

But above all the shrine cherished the sacred symbols
and pledges of the power and eternity of Rome.
Nobody knew what they were, and nobody knows to
this day, because they were only seen by the Vestal
Virgins and the Chief Priest; and for generation after
generation the secret was kept. But it was said that the
emblems were seven in number, and that they were
preserved in a large earthenware urn. They were believed to include the sacred Palladium, an effigy of

Pallas Athene (Minerva) which, according to one
popular version of its story, had been rescued by
Aeneas from the flames of Troy and brought to
Italy.[10] It had stood for the luck of Troy, but this link
had ended when Troy was no more, and now the
image represented the good fortune of Rome, and was
one of the most potent guarantors of its safety. Indeed,
this statue was so holy that the Chief Priest Lucius
Metellus was said to have gone blind when he rescued
it from a fire in the temple. But an even more dangerous moment came under the irregular emperor
Elagabalus (AD 218–22). For, desiring to make his own

Coin of Elagabalus showing the procession of his god.

Syrian god the principal divinity of Rome, he wanted
to marry that outlandish deity to Roman Vesta. With
this shatteringly untraditional idea in mind, he proposed to carry off not only the sacred fire, but the jar
containing the Palladium – so that Minerva could be
united with her eastern husband in his new Roman
shrine. But the Vestal Virgins claimed later that they
had tricked the emperor by handing over an empty
jar.[11] This story came from the current belief that, in
order to thwart such thieves, they kept two urns in
the Storehouse, one containing the Pledges and one
empty.[12]

## THE HOUSE OF THE VESTAL VIRGINS

The Virgins who guarded the shrine and all its antiquarian rituals lived a few yards away, in the House of
Vesta (Atrium Vestae). Although the fine brickwork
has been stripped of nearly all its marble facing, it is

*Above:* From the ruined House of the Vestals
the view now lies open to the Record Office (Tabularium).
*Overleaf:* The House of the Vestals.

still possible to form a good idea of what the house looked like in the first and second centuries AD when it assumed its present form.

The most extensive feature of the building was its great colonnaded courtyard which can now only be imagined from its ruined remains. The courtyards of private houses, uncovered or with a central opening over a rain-water tank, had already been adorned with Greek colonnades since *c.* 300 BC. The courtyard of this House of the Vestals beside the Roman Forum was surrounded by a portico of forty-eight columns, of which the remains are now sparse. The centre of the open space contained a garden. Three cisterns for the reception of rain-water can be seen, and in the centre there remains the outline (now largely covered) of an octagonal structure which may have been a small formal wood or thicket, the symbolic survival of some ancient grove. Under the pavement, which dates from the empire, there remain traces of its predecessor of the Republican epoch.

At the short north-western end of the court are the remains of a kitchen (with fireplace), a dining-room, and vestibule (not easily accessible today). Just outside – nearly opposite the door of Vesta's round temple – stands a chapel which, as has been said, contained a statue of the goddess. At the opposite extremity of the courtyard is a broad central chamber which corresponds to the living or reception room in private houses, but was perhaps used here as a kind of sacristy. With access to this central hall, adjoining it on either side, are six smaller rooms, formerly lined with marble. This may have been used for one of the most important functions of the building, which was to serve as a safe deposit for public and private documents, including wills. In 45 BC, the year before he was murdered, Julius Caesar deposited his will with the Vestal Virgins, and this is where it was lodged. The employment of the Vestals' house as a safe deposit is no doubt one of the principal reasons for its large size.

*Above:* The Aedicula Vestae, the shrine of the goddess outside the Temple.
*Below:* Imaginative reconstruction of the interior of the House of the Vestals.
*Opposite:* Statue of a Vestal Virgin.

The two long sides of the courtyard are flanked by a number of other small rooms. Those to the south-east, some of which were richly paved, include a small shrine; there are also the remains of a flourmill and bakery.

The courtyard, as we see it today, may date from Nero (AD 54–68), its portico and the north-western rooms from Vespasian (69–79), and the south-eastern rooms from Hadrian (117–38). In about his time, also, the building was given new back walls to protect it from damp, because the sun's rays had been shut off by grandiose structures projecting from the slopes of the Palatine nearby.

These Palatine mansions soared up from the Forum to a height of four or five storeys, and the House of the Vestals finally possessed at least two storeys of its own and probably a third. In order, therefore, to reach the requisite height, the central colonnade comprised two superimposed sets of columns, the lower ones being of green-veined 'onion' *(cipollino)* marble from Euboea, and their upper counterparts of a red-veined marble *(breccia corallina)*. Surviving portions of the house include stairs leading to the now vanished first and main

floor or, in the language of Renaissance palaces, the *piano nobile*, which was occupied by the Vestal Virgins themselves.

All round the courtyard, between the columns, are statues, or bases of statues, of Head Vestal Virgins. Those which have survived date from the third and fourth centuries AD, and were erected by the relations and friends of these Mothers Superior in gratitude for their help or protection. One of the ladies, in spite of her 'marvellous knowledge of sacrifices and holy usages', later had her name erased. She is likely to have been a Vestal who came under a curse because she went over to the Christians, perhaps in AD 365.

The Virgins wore old-fashioned long mantles of white wool, such as were otherwise only worn by brides. When sacrificing, they also put on a white hood bordered with purple, fastened on the breast with a brooch. In 420 BC a Vestal Virgin, Postumia, nearly got into serious trouble for attempting to be too *chic*; and another difficulty was her rather dubious sense of humour.

Postumia, a Vestal Virgin, was tried for incest, a crime of which she was not guilty, but suspicion had been raised by the fact that she was always got up prettily, and she had a wit which was a little too loose for a Virgin. After an adjournment she was found Not Guilty. Delivering judgement on behalf of the Board of Priests, the Chief Priest told her to stop making jokes and, in her dress and appearance, to aim at looking holy rather than smart.[13]

When a Vestal took her vows, her hair was cut off and hung on a sacred lotus tree as an offering. After it had grown again, it was dressed with six braids of artificial hair, each tied with a black and red woollen thread.

At first there were two Vestals, then four, and then normally six, divided into three seniors and three juniors. Originally all of them were patricians – that is to say, descendants of the early settlers of Rome. Later,

A Vestal Virgin from the House of the Vestals (now in the Forum Museum), one of the statues of Head Vestals erected by the supporters of these much-esteemed ladies.

plebeians were also admitted. Yet by the time of Augustus, candidates had evidently become hard to find, since he relaxed the social qualification in order to allow the enrolment of daughters of ex-slaves.

Vestals were recruited between the ages of six to ten; only children whose parents were both living were eligible. Twenty candidates were selected by the Chief Priest, and from these a single appointment was made by lot.

In early times the term of service had been only five years, but in the historical epoch Vestal Virgins were obliged to enter into a thirty-year contract. It was said that the first decade was spent learning the ceremonial, the second performing it, and the third teaching it to new recruits.

Yet Vestals were often glad to stay on after their official engagement had expired. When Occia died in AD 19 she had served for fifty-seven years, and her contemporary, Junia Torquata, achieved a record of sixty-four.

The principal duty of the Vestals was to prevent the fire in the temple of the goddess from ever going out. For at least eight hours of every twenty-four, each one of the women bore this responsibility. It was an anxious task in stormy Rome, in a small building with a single vent in its roof, to make sure that no draughts should prove fatal. If a Virgin did have the misfortune to let the fire go out, she was stripped naked and flogged by the Chief Priest himself, in the dark. And since the catastrophe could only be due to some grave personal deficiency, it was regarded as a reflection on her sexual morals.

There were edifying legends of the Vestals Aemilia and Tuccia, who had been accused of letting the fire die but proved their innocence by miracles, one igniting the cold embers by throwing a piece of linen on top of them, and the other carrying from the Tiber a sieveful of water from which not a single drop leaked. If the worst happened, and the fire went out, it had to be re-lit by rubbing wood against a cutting from a fruitful tree. The lighted tinder was then taken to the hearth in a sieve made of bronze – the earliest sacred metal, the employment of which reflects a custom going back to the Bronze Age. All this is rich material for anthropologists, who are able to suggest that the original Vestals must have been the daughters of the royal house, as in Damaraland in south-west Africa, where the chief's daughter is priestess of the perpetual fire.

If there was a constant danger of the fire going out, there was also the grave peril of the whole building catching alight, as it several times did. This hazard was all the more frightening because some of the precious Pledges in the Storehouse were surely made of wood: including the primitive Palladium itself.

If the temple caught fire, the flames must not be extinguished by water from the river or its tributaries or from artificial channels, because the Vestals (in spite of Tuccia's triumph) were not usually allowed to employ these resources. Their normal household water-supply, which one of them drew every day, came from a spring outside the city's south-eastern gate, dedicated to obscure water deities.[14] The Vestal assigned the duty for the day had to pour this water into a jar which she then carried home on her head, depositing it upon arrival in a special marble tank. On the way, she must not put it down on the ground, since the water would then have lost its virtue. To guard against this, the jars were specially made with narrow bottoms so that they could not stand.

Generally speaking, the Virgins had to perform their Kafkaesque tasks with the simplest utensils, mostly made of plain and humble earthenware. Such, for example, was the clay pot in which they baked the salt that was used for ritual purifications. It had been pounded in a mortar of archaic pattern and reduced to a hard lump, which was then cut up with an iron saw: this particular part of the rites cannot have been of the very remotest antiquity since it evidently post-dates the Bronze Age. The salt was then lodged in the Temple until the time came to mix it with flour to bake the salted cakes. This flour was made from the very first ears of ripened grain, which had been picked on odd-numbered days in the second week of May by the three Senior Vestals. The cakes were eaten at the June Festival of Vesta as well as on other sacred occasions in September and February.

After all this, it is not surprising to learn that, when the time came to clean out the Temple of Vesta, the Virgins were obliged to use special mops.

If one of these women fell ill, the Board of Priests sent her to a selected private household to receive medical attention. It had to be a home presided over by a respectable matron. Otherwise, Vestals were not allowed to leave the House except on official business.

Occasionally, however, their duties included an excursion. On 15 May of each year they went to the ancient Sublician Bridge and threw straw puppets into the Tiber. Admittedly there was something gloomy about this rite. For some reason, which had already been lost sight of in very early times, the puppets were made to represent men bound hand and foot, and Jupiter's priestess, who was in attendance, wore mourning. But at least the occasion meant a day out for the Vestals. They also attended public entertainments, including the spectacles at which gladiators slaughtered each other and wild beasts were massacred; at the Colosseum they shared the front places with the senators, sitting with the ladies of the imperial house.

We also happen to have a record of a dinner-party which some of them attended in 69 BC. Its purpose was to celebrate the installation of a new Priest of Mars.[15] The Vestals present were the four highest in rank, the other two being left behind to look after the

Vestal Virgins at a banquet; from a relief believed to belong to the altar of the Piety of the Emperor (Tiberius, AD 22). At public entertainments or celebrations Vestals were accorded the same honour as the ladies of the imperial household. Capitoline Museum.

sacred fire. The priests reclined at two tables, and two more were occupied by the ladies, who included also the new priest's wife and mother-in-law. There were thirty dishes, including a great deal of sea-food, thrushes with asparagus, and a composite main dish of sows' udders, pig's head, fricassee of fish, hare and two kinds of duck.

This, then, was an opportunity for the Vestal Virgins to relax slightly from the alarming stringency of their daily duties. But the main compensations were an excellent financial position, and their unique status in the community. It was rather as if there were only six nuns in the world, all of them living together at the very centre of power. Unlike other women, they were emancipated from the authority of the head of their own family, and possessed legal independence. On appointment, they received, in lieu of dowries, state subsidies of substantial size. In the early empire one girl was given two million sesterces, which were the equivalent of at least a hundred thousand pounds – and even a failed candidate received half that sum.

The Vestals took precedence over every other woman except the empress, and shared with her alone the privilege of travelling round Rome in a carriage. When they were on one of these journeys, they were accompanied by an official attendant; and even a consul had to make way for them in the street. Like the Priest of Mars, they were exempted from the obligation to take an oath in court.

Their patronage was enormous. If they chanced to meet a prisoner on his way to execution, they could

annul his sentence. When the youthful Julius Caesar was threatened with death at the hands of Sulla, it was they who saved his life. When Messalina was, deservedly, in terrible trouble with her husband Claudius, it was the Vestal abbess who was approached to intercede with the emperor. When Vitellius, in the Civil War of AD 69, wanted to parley with Vespasian's general, he entrusted his letter to the Vestals. When Septimius Severus launched his *coup d'état* in 193, the delegation sent from Rome to talk with him included Vestals as well as senators and priests.

And yet, in spite of these impressive missions, they were still thought of, under the later empire, as the very incarnation of the monastic retirement which was at that time coming increasingly into fashion. And above all, then as at all previous epochs, they remained the supreme symbols of Roman womanhood, and of womanly grace and beneficence. This meant that, in imperial times, there was a close equation between them and the ladies of the emperor's house – and the highest honour that any imperial lady could receive was admission to Vestal rank.[16] Furthermore, when these empresses and princesses were dead and declared to be goddesses, it was the Vestal Virgins who directed their cults. The religious revolutionary, Elagabalus, interpreted these links between empresses and Vestals in his own peculiar way. Wanting to express in earthly terms the union between his Syrian god and Roman Vesta, he actually took a Vestal Virgin out of the House and married her. She was

Coin showing Aquilia Severa, the Vestal; Elagabalus' wife.

Aquilia Severa; he divorced her quite soon, but then he married her again.[17]

This abduction must have caused profound shock, because it meant that Aquilia had to be dispensed from her vows of chastity. Complete sexual abstinence was an imperative feature of a Vestal's life. Indeed, even after their term of office was over, they rarely got married, since there was a widespread superstition that the results would be unhappy. If, while still Vestals, they were caught having sexual relations with

a man, he was flogged to death like a slave, with his head in a wooden fork, and she was buried alive in an underground chamber beneath the Field of Criminals at Rome's north gate.[18]

## THE CHIEF PRIEST'S HOUSE AND OFFICE

Somewhere in the House of the Vestals, or immediately adjoining it, lived the Chief Priest who was their administrative and spiritual superior. But this arrangement did not outlast the Republic, for after Augustus had been appointed to the Chief Priesthood, thus setting a precedent to future emperors and subsequently Popes, he moved this official residence, the Domus Publica, to the imperial quarter he had established on the Palatine. Before that, the Chief Priest's house had probably occupied a large part of the site now filled by the House of the Vestals, where floor mosaics and faint traces of painting still testify to its former existence.

This was the mansion into which Julius Caesar had moved after his surprise election as Chief Priest (63 BC), which enabled him to leave his cramped family home in the Subura. It was here, too, that a major scandal occurred in the following year when the demagogue Clodius was found masquerading as a female worshipper at the religious festival of an ancient deity known as the Good Goddess. This was a ceremony reserved for women – and rumour declared that they got disgracefully drunk on these occasions. Clodius' aim, it was asserted, was to go to bed with Caesar's wife, whom Caesar thereupon promptly divorced, with a variously reported epigram about his wife needing to be above suspicion – as he himself, although Chief Priest, emphatically was not. But the whole thing may have been a put-up job by his mother, who was glad of an opportunity to get rid of her daughter-in-law.

The residence of the Chief Priest (until Augustus moved it) immediately adjoined the building which contained the special holy place where he performed

The legendary king Numa Pompilius: statue of the early second century AD from the House of the Vestals, where a copy is now to be seen. The statue is based on an earlier model. Forum Museum.

his official duties. This curious little edifice, the Regia, was thought of as connected with the adjacent Temple of Vesta and House of the Vestals; and indeed it was apparently enclosed within the same precinct as they were, retaining the antique orientation by the points of the compass.

The remains of this structure are hard to see or understand at present, because important excavations, conducted by Professor Frank Brown, are still under way; no doubt the site will in due course be cleared up and made to look more comprehensible. The building is of complex shape. One portion of it is a small temple-like edifice which was once roofed and preceded by a porch. Next comes an irregularly oblong section comprising three compartments or courtyards, none of which ever had a roof; one of these little enclosures contains a round base.

The ancient name of this building, the Regia, suggested to the Romans that it had originally been the home of their early kings, beginning with Numa Pompilius,[19] to whom so many early religious institutions were ascribed. A copy of his statue is still in the House of the Vestals nearby (though the surviving version does not date before imperial times.) In fact, however, in the remote eighth century BC in which Numa was supposed to have lived, this area round the Forum had still been an uninhabited marsh. Yet, once the zone had been occupied and the surrounding hill-villages were merged, it appears that the Regia provided a throne-room for the kings of the unified town. Next, when the monarchy was displaced by the Republic and the headship of the religion passed to the Chief Priest, this was where he conducted his official business, including many important rites.

As a reminder of the old days, one of the chief subordinates of the Chief Priest always retained the title of 'king'. This was the *rex sacrorum*, who inherited some of the ritual functions of the monarchs and continued to perform certain acts of worship at the Regia, including ancient ceremonies connected with the King's Door.

A very early Regia, to judge from the excavations, lay below the later building, on the side nearest to the Forum. It consisted of a number of small separate constructions with stone foundations. They were built immediately on top of earlier huts, and stood within an open precinct. Finds on and near the spot suggest that these first identifiable components of the Regia were erected in *c.* 575 BC, just at the time when the

Forum was becoming the main square. The object discovered include not only pottery but terracott architectural facings which no doubt decorate wooden or mud-brick walls and simple porches. At later date these sacred places were demolished and re placed by two buildings of a more permanent nature made, in part at least, of the earliest form of volcani stone used in the city. They stood side by side an faced north; at least one of them had a front porc opening onto the Sacred Way.

In 36 BC the Regia was reconstructed by Calvinus, general of the triumvir Octavian (the later Augustus) from the proceeds of an ill-deserved Triumph won fo operations in Spain. It was probably Calvinus wh made the Regia into a single structure (though sti preserving the old duality in its two distinct parts), an who detached it from the remainder of the precinc And it was he too, apparently, who became responsib for the present curious shape of the building, whic manages to combine the old cardinal orientatio (according to the points of the compass) with the nev one the Forum had assumed. The exterior of th roofed section of Calvinus' building – the portio which now followed the new orientation – can be see from surviving fragments to have possessed fals windows and pilasters engaged in the walls and joine

A corner of the entablature from the Regia, the office of the Chief Priest, believed by the Romans to have been the home of their early kings.

direct to their lintel without capitals. Above the lintel was a frieze with a relief of garlands supported by the skulls of oxen, which were emblems believed to ward off evil.

This architectural decoration is not really worthy, artistically speaking, of the budding Augustan Renaissance. Nevertheless, when a great deal more, in excellent preservation, was uncovered in the sixteenth century, its elegance created a considerable impression – though not enough to save it from destruction. Some of the marble facings found at that time may have belonged, not to the reconstruction by Calvinus, but to further rebuilding after the fires under Nero (AD 64) and Commodus (191).

The uses to which the various small chambers were put cannot now be identified. One of them, perhaps the court containing the circular base, may have been a shrine of Mars whose sacred shield was said to have fallen from heaven and landed here in 'Numa's House'. Since an oracle declared that the seat of empire would lie wherever this shield might be, Numa was believed to have had eleven replicas made so that no one should be able to identify and remove the original. The shield of Mars was formed like the figure 8, indicating that it went back to the Bronze Age when Cretan and Mycenaean shields both had this shape.

Sacred shields (*Ancilia*) associated with the Regia and Numa Pompilius, on a copper coin of Antoninus Pius (AD 143–4).

Whenever war was declared, Roman generals aroused the power of the god by clashing the shields together and crying 'Mars, awake!' Every year, too, on his annual festival on 1 March when the fighting season was about to begin (until 153 BC this date was New Year's Day), his priests the Salii leapt through the city in a war-dance, brandishing these revered objects on their arms as they pranced.[20] Like other Roman customs, this persisted, in a characteristic blend of unbelief, half-belief and patriotic antiquarian observance; though the Hymn of the Salii was already unintelligible by the Republican age – even to the priests themselves.

The ceremony was potent war-magic, to prepare the people for the human and spiritual perils of the summer's fighting. In October, the shields were put away again. This timetable was a symbolic imitation of the procedure of war in which the archaic inhabitants of this frontier fortress spent half of every year. With the shields were associated holy spears planted in the ground. When an earthquake was imminent, they shook and trembled, and it was held that they did the same when war was on the point of breaking out.

Mars, as a high Italian god, had originally been the power of agriculture as well as war, since these were the two main occupations of the primitive community. By the same token, another of the chapels at the Regia was dedicated to Ops, the power of Plenty and Storage. This little shrine was the scene of her annual harvest ceremony on 25 August. By then a Roman harvest is in: the lower-lying ground has yielded its wheat by 31 July, and the hilly districts a little later. And so the Chief Priest and Vestals – but no one else – attended these rites symbolizing the storage of the state crops. A second ceremony of Ops, on 19 December, is rather more obscure (and indeed she, and everything about her, was already mysterious in ancient times). This ritual could have a relation to the gathering of the latest olives of the year. Or it might be linked with the idea formed by the Romans, as they personified their divine powers under Greek influence, that Ops was Rhea, the wife of Saturn, whose festival, the Saturnalia, was under way at this same season (see p. 81). Her own name, in the form of Ops Consiva, possessed formidable properties, because it was believed to be one of the secret talismanic names of Rome. Since her abode was in the earth, her worshippers remained seated while they invoked her, and as they worshipped they continually touched the ground.[21]

# 4. Shrines for the Gods

## THE TEMPLE OF SATURN

The last chapter described the Temple of Vesta and its precinct, and it is now necessary to consider the shrines of the other ancient divinities. Those which are visible today are the Temples of Saturn and the Dioscuri (Castor and Pollux) – with the Spring of Juturna attached – and the Portico of the Twelve Gods.

The Temple of Saturn balances the Temple of Vesta at the other end of the Forum. At this north-western corner of the open space stand eight columns, towering to a height of thirty-six feet. They are still surmounted by a considerable part of their lintel, frieze and cornice, together with a fragment of the triangular gable or pediment that rose above. Six of the columns, made of grey granite, form the facade of the temple, and the other two, of red granite, stand behind the end columns of the front row, forming a porch. The building stands high up on a lofty pedestal which had steps only at the front – a feature of Italian temples, in contrast to their Greek counterparts which normally had stairways on all four sides. Greek temples also usually had a vestibule at the back as well as in the front; whereas the Temple of Saturn, at back and sides alike, presented solid walls, only diversified by engaged half-columns. In Italian fashion, all attention is concentrated on the facade.

With the exception of the peculiar shrine of Vesta, this was reputedly the oldest sacred place in the Forum, and indeed, after the Temple of Jupiter on the Capitol,

The Temple of Saturn.

the oldest in all Rome. It was believed to stand upon the site of an earlier altar dedicated by Hercules himself, the man who became a god; and it is likely enough that there had been an open sanctuary here as early as the seventh century BC.

The present temple was said to have been started by Tarquinius Priscus (allegedly 616–578 BC) and dedicated by the dictator Titus Larcius in 497, or according to another version, 501 BC. But, whichever of these two versions is followed, the fact that the dedication date falls so soon after the traditional year of Rome's ejection of its kings (510 BC) is a little suspicious because it looks like a patriotic attempt to credit the temple to the young national Republic. The possibility cannot therefore be excluded that the completion of the building, like its commencement, really dates back as far as the monarchic period. The antiquity of the shrine was recalled in historic times by the archaic appearance of Saturn's statue, which was made of wood. The statue which, strangely, had its feet tied with wool, has disappeared, but fragmentary remnants of an early temple can still be seen. They include a very old piece of volcanic building stone – visible under the south-eastern wall – and traces of an altar, with a shallow channel to carry away the blood of sacrificial victims.

Several reconstructions followed over the centuries. One of them, defrayed by the Triumvirs' shifty general Plancus from the proceeds of Alpine campaigns (42 BC), is represented by the base of the temple and the fine masonry (travertine) with which it is faced. But the principal surviving part of the present building, its granite portico, dates from a subsequent restoration as late as the fourth century AD. As the inscription

This frieze inside the portico of the Temple of Saturn
was an ornamental relief two hundred years
older, appropriated from the nearby Forum of Trajan.

records, it was set in hand after a fire. The present
Ionic capitals date from this rebuilding; they had
originally been Corinthian. The restoration work was
shoddily done, one of the columns actually being
erected upside down. Moreover, the frieze inside the
colonnade consists of much earlier ornamental reliefs
which the restorers of the time appropriated from the
nearby Forum of Trajan, erected two hundred years
earlier. For late Roman architects, although (as we
shall see) capable of outstandingly magnificent achievements on their own account, were perfectly prepared,
like their medieval successors, to lift detailed features
from elsewhere. And in any case they must have regarded this old-fashioned sort of colonnaded construction as a quaint and almost incomprehensible
archaism.

Tradition maintained that Saturn had been an ancient
king of Rome who was welcomed to the city by the
god Janus and became the founder of a Golden Age,
to which Virgil and others nostalgically looked back.

But, above all, Saturn was believed to have introduced agriculture, and he became the deity of sowing
and of the seed. Since *satum* meant 'sown' in Latin, it
was assumed that this was the root from which his
name was derived. Nowadays this is not always accepted; an alternative theory traces the word back to
an Etruscan family name *Satre* or *Satria*, in which case
he was at first merely 'the god whom the Satre clan
worship'. Yet it was as a god of sowing that Saturn
was revered, and he was associated with divinities of
storage, Consus (probably from *condere*, to store) and
later Ops who was sometimes called Consiva, and
who, as was seen in connection with the Chief Priest's
official residence, came to be regarded as Saturn's wife
(Chapter 3, p. 73).

This idea dated from a time when Greek personifications were already in fashion; and Saturn himself
was identified with Greek Kronos. For Kronos too
had been thought of as founder of a Golden Age, and
the two gods had somewhat similar festivals. Even
at Rome, he still received sacrifice, like Hercules, in
the Greek fashion – with head uncovered, so as to
allow it to be open to the god's benign influence, in
contrast to the cautious Roman habit of muffling the
head in case the worship be nullified by seeing or
hearing a bad omen.

In c. 450 BC Rome's relations with Greece were
temporarily reduced to a minimum. But this temple
belongs to an earlier epoch when they were strong. It
may, as we have seen, date back to the monarchy which
was in constant touch with Greece. But even if, as
tradition maintained, the shrine was founded later on –
after 500, when the Republic had already taken over –
that was still a time when the Hellenic link remained as
strong as it had been before. There is record, during
the first half of the fifth century, of Greek artists at
Rome, corn imports from Greek Sicily, and the dis-
patch of Roman envoys to Athens – then at the height
of its culture – in order to study Athenian law. And
finds of Greek pottery in the Forum, as well as elsewhere in Rome, confirm the existence of such contacts.

Saturn was not only indebted to Kronos for pleasant
associations with the Golden Age. He also owed the
same god a sinister element in his character. The Greek

*Opposite*: The three surviving columns of the Temple of
Castor and Pollux above the steps of the Basilica Julia.
*Overleaf*: The Temple of Vesta; the Palatine Hill rises on
the right.

deity had a grim reputation, not wholly free from rumours of human sacrifice.[1] It was in keeping with these associates that Saturn's cult partner (for Roman deities were often worshipped in pairs) was Lua, who was named after *lues*, meaning plague, pestilence and calamity, and had no doubt originally been regarded as the power which brought blight and evil to the crops.

This evil, destructive aspect of Saturn was probably what caused his name, unlike those of most other gods, to be strangely shunned on the Roman coinage. The issues of the Republic display his head together with the sickle or reaping hook which was his symbol. But unlike other gods he was always left unnamed. Then there is a long interval of time in which even his figure hardly appears. Finally, in the very last century of paganism, he is seen again, still unnamed, but more often than ever before. His figure is now sometimes described as AETERNITAS, since he stands for the eternity of Rome, that concept which gained in emotional intensity during the third century AD, even though the cults of the Olympians were fading.

Saturn stood for Eternity because from a very early date his Greek counterpart Kronos had, wrongly but confidently, been identified with Chronos (Time). With its devotion to astrology, the late Roman age revered Time, or Aeon, as the agent of every propitious or unpropitious movement of the heavens: and therefore as the embodiment of the Creator himself.

The Festival of Saturn, too, which centred round the temple, retained its appeal throughout the Imperial age. The Saturnalia, at first limited to 17 December and later extending to three and finally to as many as seven days, had at first been a sacrificial rite, followed by a banquet of all the farm workers – to celebrate the completion of the autumn sowing. Then, under the influence of urbanized Greek culture, the ceremony lost its agricultural character. It became an occasion for the presentation of gifts, especially wax candles and little pottery statuettes or dolls. Above all, every restriction was relaxed. The roles of slave and master were temporarily reversed; and a Lord of Misrule was appointed, like the medieval Bishop of Fools and the Twelfth Night King of the Bean.

But although this was the merriest occasion of the year, it witnessed strange happenings on the Danube at the beginning of the fourth century AD. As year followed year, the young and handsome men appointed Lords of Misrule at Durostorum (Silistra in Rumania) put on the royal robes of Saturn; and they were allowed thirty days of uncontrolled debauchery. But then, each year, they had their throats cut, at the local altar of the god. The lethal quality in Saturn was still at work. In AD 303 the young Christian Dasius refused to accept both parts of this destiny, debauchery and death alike; and he died a martyr.

The Temple of Saturn was not only the place round which the Saturnalia revolved. It also had more practical, day-to-day functions. For this building was the storage-place for the bronze tablets on which the laws of the Roman state were inscribed. At the back of the temple, holes and iron fastenings in the wall still show where these tablets were posted up.

The temple also housed the national Roman Treasury. It is as guardian of this institution that Saturn was chosen for display on many Republican coins, since their moneyers were the annually elected quaestors who at that time were the Treasury's official heads. It was probably located in rooms underneath the shrine, at the north-east end on the Forum side. No doubt the Temple of Saturn was originally chosen for this purpose because of the link of Saturn with agriculture, which was the original source of Rome's wealth: *pecunia*, money, is related to *pecus*, cattle. Then the Treasury was called the Aerarium, from *aes* or bronze, of which, at the next stage, the national treasure mainly consisted. Subsequently the temple became the storage place for gold and silver ingots, and minted money, and any imported goods of particular value.

The Treasury also included a reserve section, derived from a tax on the liberation of slaves. During the Civil War between Caesar and Pompey, the supporters of the latter, evacuating Rome in a panic, had disastrously failed to take this national reserve with them (49 BC). But when Caesar arrived in Rome and assumed control, he made no such mistake. A tribune of the people, Lucius Metellus, courageously tried to stop him, and stood in the way before the locked gate. Metellus explained to Caesar that according to immemorial tradition the reserve could only be used for

The Temple of Antoninus and Faustina.

fighting against the Gauls. But at this point Caesar, who had spent eight years stamping out Gaulish freedom, lost patience: 'Young man!' he said, 'I've a good mind to make an end of you. You might not realize it, but I should find the action even easier than the threat.' Metellus was brushed aside, and Caesar removed 15,000 bars of gold, 30,000 bars of silver, and 30 million sesterces of coined money – this last sum being the equivalent of one and a half million pounds or more.

## THE TEMPLE OF CASTOR AND POLLUX

Balancing the Temple of Saturn at the other end of the Forum was the scarcely less ancient Temple of Castor and Pollux (Polydeuces), the divine twins known as the Dioscuri. This shrine is represented today by three graceful columns of marble from Mount Pentelicon near Athens. They rise to a height of forty-one feet, and are still surmounted by their section of horizontal entablature, including the projecting cornice. The Corinthian capitals have interlocking inner spirals which were imitated at Heliopolis (Baalbek), and then by James Gibb at St Martin's-in-the-Fields in London, and on the facade of the Cambridge Senate-House.

The columns of the Temple of Castor and Pollux are the most famous sight in the whole of the Forum. Originally they formed part of a huge colonnade which completely surrounded the inner shrine. This encasement of the building abandoned the old Italian box-like formula seen in the Temple of Saturn. But the deep frontal porch, unrepeated at the back, was still characteristic of Italian rather than Greek ideas, and so is the lofty pedestal, of which the concrete core has survived.

The facade was, at one time, approached from the ground by a central flight of steps, now demolished but still visible in a photograph taken in 1871. How-

*Opposite:* The Temple of Castor and Pollux.
*Below:* An imaginative reconstruction of the east side of the Temple of Castor and Pollux, with its inner shrine surrounded by a vast colonnade.

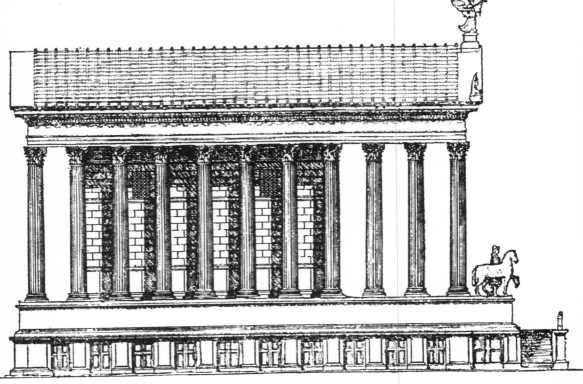

Relief of one of the Dioscuri (Castor or Pollux) with
his horse; in the Guard-room of the Palace of Domitian
(Church of Santa Maria Antiqua).

ever, this central staircase, rising from ground level, did not go back to the original arrangement. At an earlier stage, the approach to the temple from the ground was not by a frontal flight at all, but by two lateral staircases, one on either flank. They led up to a wide balustraded platform; and it was only from this higher level that there rose a broad central staircase, consisting of ten steps.

Like the shrine of Saturn this temple, contrary to Roman belief, may have gone back to the time of the kings rather than merely to the earliest days of the Republic, since the site lies within the ritual borders of the primitive village which had stood on the adjacent Palatine hill. According to the accepted tradition, however, the temple belongs to the same shadowy epoch as the temple of Saturn, transitional between monarchy and Republic. In those difficult days, it was said, the Latins supported the ejected tyrant Tarquinius Superbus and fought against the Romans in 499 or 496 BC at Lake Regillus, fourteen miles away from the city (the lake was drained in the seventeenth century). Before news of the battle had reached Rome, two young warriors were seen in the Forum, watering their white horses at the Spring of Juturna beside the site where this temple was later founded. The legend has been immortalized by Macaulay in his *Lays of Ancient Rome*. Before vanishing from the eyes of men, the horsemen announced a great victory; and in this they themselves had played the leading part. The Romans understood who their visitors had been, and built this temple for their worship, dedicating it in 484 BC.

The battle was no doubt a historical fact. It appears to have been fought at Pantano Secco beside the lake. The engagement does not, however, seem to have been the glorious one-sided victory of Roman saga. But it resulted in a memorable treaty between Rome on the one hand and the thirty Latin cities on the other – an agreement which lasted until the Latins were absorbed into the Roman state in 338 BC. A bronze copy of the treaty still survived in the Forum four centuries later.

Blocks of a type of stone dating from early times represent traces of an ancient temple. The antiquity of the cult is also suggested by a find at the neighbouring Spring of Juturna, where the Dioscuri were said to have watered their horses: the discovery consisted of fragments of archaic statues of the twin gods, copied from Greek works of the early fifth century BC.[2]

In 117 BC Lucius Metellus Delmaticus devoted much of the booty he had captured from Dalmatian pirates to an important reconstruction of the Temple of Castor and Pollux. He probably decorated the platform with the beaks of their captured ships. A floor mosaic dating from about this time has been unearthed, and it was now, also, that the base of the shrine was re-made, using the revolutionary material of concrete which had made many new developments possible since its appearance a few years earlier at the Temple of Concord across the Forum.[3]

In 70 BC Cicero accused his political enemy Verres of merely re-stuccoing one of the columns of the temple when he had undertaken to replace the stone itself.[4] Then, under Augustus, the emperor's stepson and heir, Tiberius, elaborately restored the shrine again, dedicating it in the name of himself and his dead brother Drusus the elder. The surviving columns and architectural decoration may well belong to this phase, though an alternative theory prefers to attribute them to yet another reconstruction towards the end of the first century AD.

In Republican and Imperial Rome alike Castor and Pollux were held in deep and special reverence – especially the former, whose name was often used to describe both the twins. The coinage of the early second century BC was dominated by their equestrian figures; and their popularity is corroborated by the oaths commonly taken in their names, *mecastor*, *ecastor*, *pol*, and *edepol*, the two first, in the name of Castor, being employed at first only, or mainly, by women but later by men as well.

This veneration felt for the divine brothers continued under the Empire until almost the very end of antiquity. Its persistence is demonstrated by the attention paid to the anniversaries of their shrine. Tiberius' reconstruction significantly took place in the year following what, according to one reckoning (496 BC), was the half-millenary of Regillus and the vowing of the temple; and the very first time that the name of Castor ever received specific mention on a coin was in AD 200–2, when the seven-hundredth anniversary of the other date assigned to those events (499 BC) fell due.[5] Even as late as the reign of Constantius II (AD 337–61), when the empire was officially Christian, a threat of famine induced Rome's city prefect to visit Ostia's Temple of Castor and Pollux which was one of the leading shrines in that harbour town. And then, while he was sacrificing, 'a calm smoothed the sea', according to the pagan historian Ammianus, 'the wind changed to a gentle southern breeze, and the ships entered the port under full sail and once more crammed the storehouses with grain.'[6]

This story provides a key to the character of the Greek Dioscuri as they had been envisaged in the remote past. Appearing as revered mortals in Homeric epic, they became known as the divine protectors of mariners, the gods who rescued those in peril on the sea. They were depicted with stars over their heads because they are the twin lights of St Elmo's Fire, the electrical glow which plays upon the masts of ships in stormy weather. But they had also been splendid fighters on land, and the story of their presence at Lake Regillus is directly copied from a Greek tale of a battle on the River Allaro (the ancient Sagras) in south Italy, where the people of Locri, fighting against Croton, had borrowed the aid of the twin gods from their birth-place in Greece itself, which was Sparta.[7] From Greek south Italy the cult came to the neighbourhood of Lake Regillus and also to Tusculum and Lavinium. From one or both of these towns it could easily have been passed on to Rome.

In Rome, the main feature of the ritual of Castor and Pollux was a close association with the social order of the Knights, who paraded in front of the temple every four years. By the time of Augustus, their original function as cavalry had long since vanished; but he took steps to make their younger members into a patriotic youth organization supporting the regime. The parade was now made annual. It took place on 15 July, the traditional anniversary of the battle of Lake Regillus, and the knights came in from the Temple of Mars outside the city wearing rich clothes and olive garlands and carrying trophies.

The large tribunal in front of the Temple of Castor and Pollux was originally intended for the taking of the salute at this parade. At first it may have existed as a separate platform. This may also have been the place where, from the fourth century BC onwards, officials conducted the public gatherings *(contiones)* preliminary to the official vote-taking meetings of the Assembly in which the Roman people, under the name of the Comitia Tributa, was marshalled in its ancient divisions known as tribes. For a long time the actual balloting still continued to take place elsewhere, at the Old Rostra in the Comitium at the other end of the Forum

(Chapter 6, pp. 110–112). But owing to a shortage of space in that cramped area, this balloting was transferred from the Comitium in 145 BC to the place where the preliminary meetings had already perhaps been held for two hundred years – the 'centre of the Forum';[8] that is to say, the tribunal in front of the Temple of Castor.

In 117 BC the platform was reconstructed and made into an organic part of the temple's facade. The voters marched up onto the dais two by two on temporary wooden gangways, and then after they had registered their votes they descended again by the two unusual stone side-staircases which had now been constructed for this purpose. Other wooden structures besides the gangways may also have been erected on these occasions to extend the size of the platform.

This tribunal is also likely to have been the place specified as the spot where magistrates took the oath to abide by the laws.[9] Nevertheless, it was here also that Sulla sat to watch one of his centurions murder a candidate for the consulship whom he did not like.

Cicero speaks of the Temple of Castor and Pollux as 'that famous and glorious monument of the past, that sanctuary which stands where the eyes of the nation may rest on it every day'.[10] Nevertheless, it witnessed deplorable scenes of melodrama and violence during the last years of the Republic. Sulla used its entrance as a barricade. In 62 BC Caesar and a tribune, Quintus Metellus Nepos, wanted to pass a bill there in order to bring Pompey back from the east with his army, but Cato would have none of it. Instead, 'seeing the Temple of Castor and Pollux encompassed with armed men, and the steps guarded by the gladiators, and at the top Metellus Nepos and Caesar sitting together', Cato shoved his way through with a colleague, and sat forcibly between them, 'at which both of them were amazed and confounded'.[11] Then he snatched Nepos' documents out of his hand, but as stones and cudgel-blows rained down upon him he had to be led away to take refuge inside the temple.

Three years later Caesar, as consul, passed his highly controversial first agrarian law on this same platform, but not before his fellow-consul Bibulus, breaking through the guards, had mounted the steps in order to try to interrupt, with the result that he had a basket of excrement emptied over his head and was beaten up. In the following year the gangster-tribune Clodius assembled his thugs and weapons in the temple, and demolished the stone steps to keep everyone else out.

His colleague Sestius was wounded here, and Cicero, who makes repeated references to all this, describes the arrest, on the same spot, of a slave whom Clodius had commissioned to murder Pompey.[12]

Such events, combined with the evil reputation of the adjoining Tuscan Street, cannot have been very encouraging to the many citizens who used the vaults of the Temple as a safe deposit like the adjoining House of the Vestals. The government itself did the same, and also hung bronze copies of treaties on the outer wall. In the basement, too, was Rome's Bureau of Standards, an office for the testing of weights and measures. The main testing centre was on the Capitoline Hill,[13] but the office in the Temple of Castor and Pollux may have been a branch intended for the convenience of local jewellers and metal-workers.

The deranged or at least eccentric emperor Caligula (AD 37–41) gave a temporary, if somewhat blasphemous, additional distinction to the temple. 'He built out a part of the Palatine palace as far as the Forum, and making the Temple of Castor and Pollux its vesti-bule, he often took his place between the divine brethren, and exhibited himself there to be worshipped by those who presented themselves.'[14] Jokingly, or half-jokingly (it was hazardous to treat what he said as entirely a joke), he observed that the divine brethren thus became his doorkeepers. But his structure, which projected westwards into the Forum on a grandiose scale,[15] was destroyed by fire only forty years later.

## THE SPRING OF JUTURNA

Beside the surviving columns on the south-east flank of the Temple of Castor and Pollux is the Spring of Juturna (Lacus Juturnae), at which the brothers were said to have watered their horses after the battle of

The Spring of Juturna (Lacus Juturnae), converted by the Romans into a square monument (right foreground). The central rectangular base has lost its statues.

*Above:* Altar of Castor and Pollux; found at the Spring of
Juturna, where a copy now stands. Forum Museum.
*Opposite:* Female figure on the altar of Castor and Pollux,
possibly Helen.

Lake Regillus. The spring was converted into a monument in the form of a square basin made of diamond-shaped bricks faced with marble.[16]

In the centre of the basin is a rectangular marble-faced base. The statues that surmounted it have gone, but perhaps they were the copies of fifth-century BC Greek figures of Castor and Pollux, of which fragments have been found here (p. 85). The travertine balustrade of imperial date which runs round three sides of the basin now display a copy of another local find, a marble altar. On its main sides are reliefs of Castor and Pollux and their sister Helen (?), and at the short ends their mother Leda with her swan, and Jupiter with his sceptre and thunderbolt. The altar, which is perhaps of the second century AD, may have formed part of this monument of Juturna, or it may have belonged to the Temple of Castor and Pollux next door.

To the south of the spring is Juturna's shrine, with brick walls fronted by a little porch of two Corinthian columns crowned by a gable; an inscription on the lintel bears the name of the goddess. The shrine, now reconstructed with modern travertine additions,

The Shrine of Juturna (restored).

originally contained her statue. In front of this structure, covering the mouth of a well, is a marble well-head dedicated to her by a city official who perhaps lived in the time of Augustus.[17] Before the well-head stands an altar engraved with figures of Juturna and her brother Turnus.

In ancient times these waters were drunk for thei medicinal qualities, and between the spring and a ramp leading up to the Palatine are the ruins of room designed for the accommodation of ancient Roman taking the cure. The remains that still exist date from the later empire, when the city's water administration was established here; an inscription bearing a dedica tion to Constantine by its director has survived. One large room has a black and white mosaic depicting aquatic scenes. The numerous other finds on the site include a statue of the god of healing, Aesculapius with his page, and an archaic torso of Apollo, who wa the father of Aesculapius and, like him, was believed to possess supreme curative powers. There was a cul of Apollo at Gabii, very close to Lake Regillus, where Castor and Pollux were believed to have fought in the battle before coming to this spring (p. 85).

The worship of Juturna herself, however, seems to have been brought to Rome from Lavinium. The origin of her name is disputed, but she was a power o spirit of water-springs, entrusted by Jupiter with the care of lakes and rivers, as a reward for a love-affair.[1] Virgil, who offers this version, also made her the siste of the tragic Italian, Turnus, whom Aeneas killed This sort of story is relatively late, and indeed the cul of Juturna did not become really fashionable until the First Punic War (241 BC), when the Romans con fronted with the need to fight naval battles, honoured her as one of the water-deities to whom they vowed temples in various parts of Rome. She received anothe temple from Augustus, and it is from that time probably, that a festival was held in her honour, in which all who used water in their daily work could take part.

The water from this ancient spring beside the Forum, being situated so close to great temples, was habitually used for religious sacrifices; and when there was a drought, the spring itself became the object o sacrifices and prayers, offered in the hope that the rains would be renewed.

## THE PORTICO OF THE TWELVE GODS

The latest in date of all surviving sanctuaries of pagan deities lies on the other side of the Forum, nestling into the angle of the Capitoline Hill. This is the Portico of the Twelve Gods. These *Di Consentes e Complices*[19] – perhaps meaning the 'agreeing' o 'harmonious' gods – comprised the most importan

The Portico of the Twelve Gods;
behind, the Record Office (Tabularium); to the right
the Temple of Vespasian.

Olympians, namely Jupiter and his divine Council. The early Latin poet Ennius managed, by using the antique form 'Jovis' for 'Jupiter', to fit the names of all twelve into two lines of hexameter verse.

The portico, which stands on an artificially levelled terrace, consists of small columns of Euboean *cipollino* marble, of which nine survive, supplemented by modern pieces of travertine. They are surmounted by Corinthian capitals decorated with trophies. Above these, the lintel, frieze, and part of the cornice are still intact. The colonnade forms two sides of an obtuse angle. Beneath it lie unidentifiable rooms, and behind the portico itself are seven small chapels or chambers built onto the hill, five on the flank and two at the rear; perhaps they were originally twelve, providing a shrine for each of the divinities. This is where the gilded statues of the Twelve Gods, referred to by the antiquarian Varro, must have been. Presumably they stood within the little chapels.[20]

The original portico may have dated from the Second Punic War. For after the Romans had suffered a disastrous defeat from the Carthaginians at Lake Trasimene (217 BC), one of the various propitiatory ceremonies decreed was a Sacred Banquet at which the Twelve Gods were made guests at a ceremonial meal, couches being prepared for them as for human diners, with one male and one female deity at each couch.[21] This may have been the occasion when the Portico was first dedicated and built somewhere in or near the Forum, though it may not have been moved to this particular site until later. In any case nothing of the early structure survives. Some of the brickwork seems to belong to the time of Vespasian (AD 69–79) or his son Titus, whose temple the portico adjoins. But an inscription above the columns indicates that virtually the whole building, as we see it, is a reconstruction undertaken by the city prefect Vettius Agorius Praetextatus in AD 367.

The fact that the restoration of a pagan shrine took place at so very late an epoch is of considerable interest. The empire had been officially Christian since the time of Constantine the Great (306–37), with only a brief reversion to paganism under his disillusioned relative Julian 'the Apostate' (361–3). At the time when the restoration of the portico was undertaken, Julian was dead and official Christianity had been re-established. But the new Christian Emperor of the West, Valentinian 1, though savage in many respects, was unusually tolerant in religious matters,[22] and paganism at Rome remained very strong, especially among the nobility. It was not until later in the century that more decisive repressions took place; as will be seen when we come to discuss the Senate-house in Chapter 6.

Meanwhile, one of the most determined opponents of Christianity was the learned Vettius Praetextatus, the man who restored this portico. Among the offices he held were important pagan priesthoods, and his epitaph gives these priority over all his other posts. A contemporary description of Vettius' religious attitude indicates that, like other cultured pagans of the time, he did not believe in the individual deities, but professed a monotheistic solar theology in which all gods are manifestations of a single power who is identifiable with the Sun.

To rebuild a portico honouring the leading Olympians at such a time, under a Christian emperor, was a remarkable gesture of defiance; as Alfonso Bartoli declared, this is 'a monument of the most profound religious crisis recorded in history'. It is not surprising to learn that the death of this pagan leader in 385, at a time when he was consul designate, took the heart out of the pagan opposition.

Vettius had not been above cracking a slightly malicious joke with his enemies. For the worldly power and pomp of the churchman, Damasus, inspired him to remark: 'Make me bishop of Rome, and I will become a Christian tomorrow!'

# 5. Shrines for the Caesars

## THE TEMPLE OF JULIUS CAESAR

The Forum possessed famous temples not only of the gods, but of rulers of Rome who after their deaths had been declared to be enrolled among their number. At least three of these shrines, and possibly a fourth, can be identified in the area. They are the Temples of Julius Caesar, of Vespasian and Titus, of Antoninus Pius and Faustina, and perhaps also of Romulus the son of Maxentius.

Just inside the entrance of the modern archaeological enclosure of the Forum, the Temple of Julius Caesar stood facing the short south-eastern end of the square. It was a small building with a porch only on its facade – which looked out over the Forum and provided it with a monumental closure. The porch consisted of eight Corinthian columns, six in front and two behind at either end. Not very long after the construction of the temple, an external portico was built on all its four sides. This took the form of a closed corridor at the back, but it was open at the front and on the two flanks, where it linked up with arches which spanned the adjoining streets.[1]

The inner shrine was unusual, because the constricted nature of the site required a shape much wider than it was deep. Like the Temple of Castor and Pollux, the building stands on a high base, and is fronted by an extensive platform reached by two flights of steps. Here, however, the staircases are not placed at the sides, as they are at that building, but instead pierce the front, which is also interrupted, at its central point between the two staircases, by a semicircular niche or recess containing a round stone altar.

The rubble core of the temple's base, stripped of its stone facing, still exists, but above that level nothing has survived at all. This is a site which is rewarding only for its associations, not for what there is to see. The platform, however, has been partially restored, and it is still possible to note the outline of its frontal recess, which was at one time crudely walled up but has now been re-opened so that the altar can again be seen. Fragments of the cornice are preserved, and the Forum Museum possesses two pieces of a frieze which probably belonged to the temple. It displays spiral designs and figures of divinities set among foliage. One of the two sections of the relief is much better executed than the other, but both are rather conservative in style.

The temple had its beginnings in those tumultuous days of 44 BC which followed the assassination of Julius Caesar. Its platform stands on the site of an earlier platform, to which, after that earth-shaking event, a group of men who were serving or had served in high offices of state had brought the corpse of the dictator.

The place seemed appropriate for his funeral, because it was so close to the Regia where Caesar had presided as Chief Priest. Plans to cremate him in the Temple of Jupiter on the Capitol were thwarted by its priests, and an idea of performing the rite in the hall of Pompey's Theatre in the Field of Mars, the place where he had been murdered, likewise came to nothing.[2] And so, after Antony had delivered his funeral oration at the New Rostra just across the Forum (Chapter 6), the huge disorderly crowd burnt the body on this spot, where Caesar's temple was later to be erected.

Some cried out to kill the murderers, and others, as formerly in the case of Clodius the demagogue, dragged from the shops the benches and tables, piled them upon one another, and thus constructed a huge pyre. On this they set Caesar's body, and in the midst of many sanctuaries, places of refuge and holy places, burned it. Moreover, when the fire blazed up, people rushed up from all sides, snatched up half-burnt brands, and ran round to the houses of Caesar's slayers to set them on fire.[3]

Then the ashes of the dictator were moved to his family tomb in the Field of Mars, where they were laid to rest beside his daughter Julia, who had died ten years earlier.

The round altar still to be seen in the recess before Caesar's temple marks the position where the body was burnt. It also marks the place of an earlier altar, which was set up shortly after the cremation. For in the days following the funeral a shady veterinarian called Herophilus or Amatius, who claimed to be a grandson of the great general Marius, had gained a hysterical following when he built an altar on this

spot. He also set up a twenty-foot-high column of Numidian marble, inscribed 'To the Father of his Country', a title which Caesar had favoured in his last days as an unofficial or semi-official description of his national role. This column and altar formed the first monument to mortal man ever to be erected within the precincts of the Forum. Fearing grave disorders, the consuls Antony and Dolabella, though supporters of Caesar, demolished both structures, and, as a further safety measure, executed Herophilus and the other demonstrators concerned.

Caesar's assassins met their deaths at Philippi (42 BC). Then his adopted heir Octavian, the future Augustus, held the first Funeral Games in the dictator's honour. As the celebrations got under way, 'a comet shone for seven successive days, rising about the eleventh hour, and was believed to be the soul of Caesar'.[4] And so Octavian together with Antony and Lepidus, the other members of the triumvirate which

Reconstruction of the Temple of Julius Caesar and the altar built on the place where Caesar was cremated.

was now exercising dictatorial rule, vowed a temple to his divinity.

Years later, after Lepidus had been eliminated (36 BC) and Antony and Cleopatra, defeated at the battle of Actium, had committed suicide (30), Octavian performed the dedication of the temple. He dedicated spoils of war in the shrine,[5] and the front of the dais was probably adorned, according to a tradition for such platforms, with the beaks of Cleopatra's ships captured at Actium. Augustus also lodged in the temple a famous picture of Venus (Caesar's divine ancestor) rising from the waves, painted by the great Apelles (c. 330 BC). When its condition deteriorated, Nero replaced it by a masterpiece, executed by a certain Dorotheus.

The site of Herophilus' short-lived altar, intended for the veneration of Caesar immediately after his death, was respected by the builders of the subsequent temple, who chose the same place for their erection of the round altar which is still to be seen in the central indentation of the platform.

Inside the wide shrine, standing against its back wall, rose a huge effigy of the deified Caesar. It has vanished, but we learn that it bore a flaming comet on his brow:

> To make that soul a star that burns forever
> Above the Forum and the gates of Rome.[6]

The religion of the later Greeks and of the Romans was the only one of the world's faiths in which man, if he had achieved special greatness in his lifetime, could aspire to become a god. Castor and Pollux, whose temple was just across the road, were believed to have been human beings whose glory had raised them to heaven after their deaths. And the same was asserted of another god worshipped in the vicinity, Saturn, who in earlier times had presided over a mythical Golden

The altar and Temple of Julius Caesar as they appear in the Forum today, beside the Temple of Vesta.

Age (Chapter 4, p. 76). But the classic example of the phenomenon was held to be Heracles, brought from Greece to Rome at a very early date under the name of Hercules.

The idea was adapted to Roman use by the deification of the national founder Romulus, and a philosophical basis was provided by Euhemerus of Messene (*c.* 300 BC), who claimed to have gone to a fabulous island in the Indian Sea and found there a golden column on which were written the deeds that the gods had performed while they were once upon a time living upon the earth.[7] The mighty achievements of Alexander the Great had encouraged this tendency to regard great men as gods after their death, and the subject-peoples of his successors found it an easy step to call them gods in their lifetimes. The Romans felt unable to accept this, at least as a state institution: but the extraordinary career of Caesar did cause them to come very close to making an exception in his case and regarding him as a god while he was still alive. And when he was dead, the Roman state decreed that a god was what he had now become.

Later on, when the personality cult of Roman emperors waxed great, the Greek east was not only allowed but positively encouraged to hail them as gods during their lifetimes. Yet the formal parlance of the capital still stopped just short of this. After their deaths, on the other hand – if their reigns had won favour – the custom of bestowing official godhead continued, and the Temple of Caesar looked ahead to a long line of such imperial shrines and gods. But they were revered rather than worshipped, and an emperor whom the state had raised to heaven was distinguished from the Olympians by being called *divus* instead of *deus*.

The platform of the Temple of Caesar continued to be used for impressive funerals. The body of Augustus himself was laid in state upon this dais, and it was here that his stepson and heir Tiberius delivered the principal funeral oration. 'Senators clamoured that the body of Augustus should be carried to the pyre on their own shoulders. Tiberius, with condescending leniency, excused them. He also published an edict requesting the populace not to repeat the disturbances of Caesar's funeral – due to over-enthusiasm – by pressing for Augustus to be cremated in the Forum instead of the Field of Mars, his appointed place of rest.'[8]

The choice of the dais of the Temple of Caesar for Tiberius' funeral oration in honour of Augustus re-

called that this platform had been designed as a supplement or annex of the principal public platform of the Roman state, the New Rostra, which will be described in the next chapter. In consequence of this, the temple dais was known as the Rostra ad Divi Juli. Although the Assembly of the Roman People had been reduced to permanent impotence by Augustus, it continued for a time to go through the motions of legislation, and we learn that the Rostra ad Divi Juli was used as a place where it voted,[9] perhaps, as elsewhere, with the addition of temporary wooden structures.

The temple was restored on a number of occasions, for example by Septimius Severus (AD 193–211) after the fire of 191.

## THE TEMPLE OF VESPASIAN AND TITUS

A much more conspicuous landmark is the temple of two later deified emperors, Vespasian and Titus, who died in AD 79 and 81 respectively. This building is at the other end of the Forum, on the lower slopes of the Capitoline Hill. Situated outside the modern archaeological area, it can now best be seen from the Via del Foro Romano which overlies part of the Capitoline Rise.

Three soaring, fluted columns survive, rising to a height of fifty feet. They belong to the corner of what was once a porch of eight columns (six in front), facing the Forum. Their height seems all the greater because they stand on a high pedestal, faced with stone blocks which were once covered by marble. The horizontal crown or entablature of the surviving columns still exists, including portions of a rich cornice and a frieze skilfully decorated with sacrificial implements, the symbols of the Chief Priesthood which formed part of the imperial functions. The frieze also includes representations of the skulls of oxen, held to possess powers of warding off evil. These designs can be seen at close quarters on a further extensive section of the entablature preserved in the gallery of the Record Office (Tabularium) which rises beyond the temple.

The Temple of Vespasian; behind it the Record Office (Tabularium), the substructure of the later Palace of the Senator.

Cornice and frieze of the Temple of Vespasian
decorated with the ritual implements of sacrifice and the
skulls of oxen, believed to ward off evil.
In the gallery of the Record Office.

Just inside the shrine's back wall (now vanished) there still stands a large base, which served as a pedestal for the statues of the two deified emperors. When Vespasian died, he was proclaimed a divinity of the Roman state, and his sons Titus and Domitian began the temple. Vespasian, who possessed a pawky sense of humour, took a somewhat earthy view of his inevitable future promotion to join the gods. Stricken by fatal illness, he struggled to his feet to die standing, as an emperor should, and declared: 'A pity – I believe I am turning into a god!' And so he became the next imperial *divus* after Augustus and Claudius, both of

Imaginative reconstruction of the Temple of Vespasian (centre) with the Temples of Saturn and Concord to the left and right of it.

whom he had admired. Then Titus died only two years later, and he too was raised to divinity and included in the same temple by his brother Domitian.

On its facade, the lintel surmounting the Corinthian capitals shows a fragment of an inscription including the huge letters R E S T I T V E R, part of *restituerunt*, 'they restored'. A visitor in the eighth century AD, from Einsiedeln in Switzerland, was able to inspect this inscription in its entirety, and saw that it identified the restorers of the temple as Septimius Severus (193– 211) and Caracalla. Like Vespasian, Severus was trying to form a dynasty, and he welcomed the opportunity to revive the memory of a father-son partnership that had been so successful and popular as that of Vespasian

and Titus – especially as it must have been clear that his own son Caracalla was turning out to be a horror. Besides, deified emperors of the past were especially revered at military camps, and Severus respected the feelings of the army more meticulously than any other emperor ever had before.

Even when paganism began to wane and the Olympians seemed less interesting, former rulers who had become *divi* continued to receive veneration as generalized concepts of the glorious, patriotic tradition of Rome. And so, forty years after Severus, when the affairs of the empire looked thoroughly bleak, one of his desperate successors issued a series of coins commemorating the entire gallery of his divine predecessors;[10] and Vespasian and Titus duly appear among them.

## THE TEMPLE OF ANTONINUS AND FAUSTINA

On the other side of the Forum, next to the Temple of Caesar, rises the shrine of a further pair of imperial divinities, this time not two emperors but an emperor and an empress, Antoninus Pius (AD 138–161) and his wife, Faustina the elder. This is the best preserved monument of the entire area, a distinction which it owes to its subsequent incorporation in the church of St Lawrence (S. Lorenzo in Miranda). In front of the present baroque facade of the church, which stands considerably above the ancient ground-level, rises the Roman temple's deep porch, made of ten unfluted sixty-five foot high columns of green-veined Euboean *cipollino* marble, six on the facade and two more behind at each end, the two hindmost on either side forming the frontal extremities of the side-walls. Originally these walls also contained engaged columns along their entire length, but these, like the marble wall-facings, have now disappeared. However, the side-walls themselves still remain intact, constructed of massive pepper-coloured stone blocks *(peperino)* from beside Lake Albano.[11]

The lofty substructure is mounted by a fine frontal flight of twenty-one steps, now restored. Half way up the steps are the remains of an altar. At the top, within the colonnade, stood colossal statues, of which fragments are preserved; they were presumably effigies of the deified imperial couple.

On both flanks of the exterior, running along the top of the porch and of the side walls, a particularly

Coin of Antoninus showing his Temple.
*Below:* The Temple of Antoninus and Faustina in a
water-colour by L. F. Cassas (1756–1827). Graphische
Sammlung, Albertina, Vienna.
*Opposite:* The Temple of Antoninus and Faustina today.

well executed frieze is still to be seen. It shows a series of griffins facing one another in pairs, with a candelabrum between each beast and the next. Griffins were sacred to Apollo and reminiscent of the art of the Augustan age, a period for which Antoninus felt an antiquarian admiration. These heraldic beasts continued to appear on sarcophagi and other funeral monuments. Sometimes they represent the means of transit for the conveyance of the dead person's soul to the gods. But here they guard the fire that purifies and sanctifies the dead, in the spirit of the solar worship which was continually gaining ground until it almost monopolized later paganism and became mingled with the rising faith of Christianity.

Soon after the beginning of the long and peaceful reign of Antoninus Pius, his wife Faustina died. She was deified, and this temple was erected in her memory. By this time there was no novelty about adding a *diva* to the list of *divi*. In the early days of the institution, such a step had scarcely seemed practicable, and it was not until eighty-two years after the deification of Julius Caesar that the first Roman woman had joined him in the official heaven. Probably this caused some-

thing of a scandal at the time, since she was Drusilla, the sister of Caligula,[12] whose deep love for her was said to be incestuous. It was awkward that a much greater lady, Livia the wife of Augustus, had not received this honour when she died nine years earlier; at the time Tiberius, who had suffered a lot from his mother, rather lamely said she had never wanted the distinction. But this was rectified when Claudius deified Livia in AD 41, thus creating a proper precedent for future empresses.

Coinage was sometimes issued with portraits of imperial ladies, after their deaths as well as in their lifetimes; and it is perhaps a measure of Antoninus' devotion to Faustina that he issued an enormous, unprecedented mass of coins in honour of the new goddess. There remained, however, persistent rumours that her character had been unsatisfactory. 'Poore man!', wrote Richard Lassels in 1670, 'he could not make her an *honest woman* in her lifetime, and yet he would needs make her a *Goddesse* after her death.'

When Antoninus himself died twenty years later, he, too, was deified, and the senate decreed that the temple should be re-dedicated so as to include his name as well. The two-line inscription recording the successive dedications can still be seen on the facade, with his name added to hers at a later date.

The temple became famous, and served as a model for similar buildings elsewhere, for example at Ebora (Evora in Portugal). Its columns were also much favoured by ancient writers of *graffiti*. One of these scrawls shows the Chi-Rho monogram which was the emblem of Christ, flanked by the letters Alpha and Omega. It is believed to belong to the second half of the fourth century AD, and has been claimed as the oldest Christian relic in the Forum area.

## THE SO-CALLED TEMPLE OF ROMULUS

One other monument in this region may be conjecturally added to the list of temples dedicated to imperial deities. Again it is relatively well preserved. This is the round brick edifice known as the Temple of Romulus,

*Previous page:* The Sacred Way (Sacra Via) with the so-called Temple of Romulus on the near right.

forty yards south-east of the Temple of Antoninus and Faustina. Its marble covering has gone, and its present roof is not original either. The building was adjoined on either flank by small rectangular halls terminating in apses at their far ends. In front of each of these side halls was a porch, with two columns of *cipolline* marble; those on the right side still exist.

The facade of the central rotunda itself displays concave, niched curves foreshadowing seventeenth century baroque. Between them, the main doorway is framed by two small columns of red porphyry and surmounted, in the insouciant late Roman fashion, by a finely sculptured lintel taken from some other building. The original bronze doors are still there. Their decoration has gone, yet the doors themselves have surprisingly escaped the ravages of innumerable covetous visitors during the Middle Ages and Renaissance. Even the ancient lock is still in working order.

*Below:* The Temple of Romulus in a drawing by O. B. M. Valkenborch II (*c.* 1566–1597). Akademie der bildenden Künste, Vienna.
*Opposite:* The original bronze doors of the Temple of Romulus still stand today.

Coin of the deified Romulus showing a shrine which may represent the temple named after him beside the Forum.

This decorative triple entrance faced onto the Sacred Way, at the raised level established by Nero when he converted the street into a monumental approach leading to his Golden House (Appendix 2).

Architectural considerations indicate that the temple dates from the early fourth century AD. It bears a certain resemblance to a building shown, in two different forms, upon coins of the emperor Maxentius. These coins were issued in honour of his son Romulus, who died in boyhood and subsequently received official deification (c. 309). Maxentius himself, before he was struck down by Constantine at the battle of the Milvian Bridge (312), adopted a policy of pagan, traditional Romanism, appropriate to his re-establishment of the imperial residence at Rome itself, which had for a

generation previously ceased to be the capital of the empire. It was in accordance with this policy that he posthumously deified his youthful son. This was almost the last pagan gesture of the kind. Yet even the Christian Constantine later honoured an alleged ancestor in this same way – and was himself called *divus* after his death.[13]

Although the identification cannot be regarded as certain, this round building may be the temple of young Romulus which is shown on the coins.[14] An inscription in honour of Constantine on the facade which we know of from a sixteenth-century drawing does not rule this attribution out, because Constantine is known to have re-dedicated other buildings of Maxentius in his own name, notably the huge adjoining Basilica which will be described in the next chapter.

The Mausoleum where the young Romulus was buried has been identified on the Appian Way outside the city. That too is round; for this was an age of centralized temples and mausoleums of various interesting designs, the forerunners of Christian baptisteries.

The clever architect who designed the circular building beside the Forum wanted to mask the orientation of an older rectangular hall which stood behind it at an inconveniently oblique angle to the Sacred Way. The hall was probably the library of the Forum of Peace which Vespasian built from the spoils of the Jewish War (AD 70). It therefore belonged not to the Forum Romanum but to the adjoining Imperial Fora which are outside the scope of this book. It is, however, relevant to any study of Roman topography for a special reason, because from the time of Septimius Severus (c. AD 200) a plan of the whole city, the Forma Urbis, was affixed to its external walls; the most important fragments to come to light were found just outside the hall in 1562. The holes for the insertion of its various panels are still to be seen in the brick wall at the north-east end. Some of the discoveries later vanished, but fortunately they had first been reproduced in drawings preserved in a Vatican manuscript. Summary but comprehensive, the Forma Urbis, even in such a fragmentary form, has contributed greatly to our knowledge of certain parts of the ancient city.

The walls of this oblong hall have continued to exist because they were incorporated in the church of Saints Cosmas and Damian, and the so-called Temple of Romulus, too, has survived because it was attached to the same church as a vestibule or antechapel.

View across the Forum towards the round 'Temple
of Romulus'; in the background stands the Basilica Nova of
Maxentius and Constantine.

The 'New' Rostra and the Arch of Severus.
The Rostra is drilled with dowel-holes to hold the
decorative prows of ships.
*Opposite:* Reconstruction of the Rostra.

# 6. The Meeting Places of People and Senate

## THE ROSTRA

One of the Forum's greatest claims to fame was its function as the governmental centre of Rome and its empire, the place where the Roman orators pronounced their speeches, including Cicero, whose powers of persuasion have never been exceeded.

However, the main platform for public speaking, at least in the form in which it has come down to us, only dates from the last years of Cicero's life. This is the New Rostra, which closes the Forum's north-western end. Begun by Julius Caesar, it was completed, some years after his death, by Augustus. The platform is ten feet high, eighty long and forty deep. Its front, which is straight, has been reconstructed in modern times with small stone fragments; but a number of ancient blocks, dating from a restoration of imperial times, can still be seen at one corner. The back of the Rostra is of a curious concave shape, incorporating a wide, inwardly curved staircase of six marble steps leading up to the platform.

At one end of the staircase (NW) stands a small round brick base on which rested the Navel of Rome (Umbilicus Romae). This strange object, in the shape of a cone, represented the official, though not the geographical, centre of the city – in imitation of a Greek custom – and was probably erected by Septimius Severus. At the opposite extremity of the steps (SW) were found fragments of the Golden Milestone (Miliarium Aureum), a bronze-encased marble column set

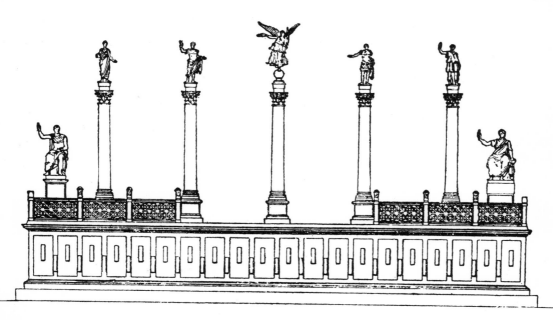

up by Augustus when he took over the care of the empire's roads in 20 BC. He inscribed it in gold letters with a record of the distances between the capital and the other chief cities of the empire.

The Rostra was transferred by Caesar to its present 'new' position from a site 150 yards away in front of the Senate-house, where the Old Rostra had stood from very ancient times. The earlier site had adjoined the Comitium, an open space measuring three hundred feet across. The Comitium had been the meeting place of some of the kings, and had subsequently become the place of assembly of the Roman people. Its long history in that capacity is reflected by excavations of no less than seven superimposed strata of Republican date.

This historical background of the Old Rostra accounts for the inward curving back of the new one: for this feature was faithfully copied from its predecessor.

The old platform had possessed this unusual shape because, while its front faced the Forum, its back rested against the edge of the Comitium, which was a circular area surrounded by steps: at one point in the circuit of the Comitium, that is to say, its curving steps served the Old Rostra as well, and formed its back. This explanation for the shape of the Rostra, Old and New, has been derived from the discovery of a similar round, stepped space at Cosa on the Etruscan coast, likewise in front of the local Senate-house. The feature may be of south Italian inspiration, since a comparable crescent of steps has also come to light at Paestum (Posidonia). Furthermore at Rome itself, in the area of the Comitium and Old Rostra, fragments of a circular stone staircase have now been found. They date back to the time of Sulla (c. 80 BC). Earlier, perhaps, the full circuit of steps did not exist; in antique times the only staircase down into the Comitium may have

An imagined scene in the Roman Forum, the foreground buildings removed to show the 'New' Rostra on the left with the Curia behind it.

been the steps descending, at one point in its circumference, from the front of the adjacent Senate-house.

One identifiable feature of the Old Rostra, however, goes back to the fourth century BC. The word means 'beaks' or prows, and the platform was called by this name because it was decorated with the bronze prows captured from defeated Latins in a naval battle at Antium (Anzio) – the victory which led to the historic federation of the Latins with Rome (338 BC).[1] The feature was perpetuated in Caesar's New Rostra (as on other public platforms) and the surviving ancient portions of its front still show holes in which the gilded beaks were fastened. Another feature which was likewise transferred from the Old Rostra to the New was a commemorative column fitted with further beaks of ships. These had been captured by Gaius Duilius, who won Rome's first naval Triumph against the Carthaginians (260 BC).

The Comitium had witnessed a great deal of Roman history, down to the day when the inflamed populace cremated the body of Clodius on an improvised funeral pyre, burning down the adjacent Senate-house. Livy refers to many happenings in the Comitium – omens, floggings, the dedications of statues – but its main purpose was to provide a meeting place for the Comitia or Assembly of the People.

Although these Assemblies were so greatly dominated by politicians and nobles that they could not be regarded as any more democratic than, say, an eighteenth-century English electorate, they remained the sovereign law-giving and elective organ of the Roman state, and contributed an enormous amount to the activity, excitement and hubbub of Republican life. And so they also supplied the supreme challenge to the oratory of Cicero, who had to give these highly excitable and irrational audiences far more vigorous fireworks than he usually thought fit to supply to the more dignified Senate.

The Comitium was believed by the ancients to date back to the time of Romulus. However, it was not, in fact, the very earliest place of Assembly under the Roman kings; for that had been a sanctuary of Vulcan behind the New Rostra (Appendix 2). But the Comitium had already replaced the Vulcanal in this capacity in very ancient times, and it was there that the Assemblies, or Comitia, of the Roman people held their meetings under the later monarchy and the subsequent Republic. The earliest Assembly, known as the Curiata, had been made up of thirty *curiae*, or groups of families. In historical times, under the presidency of the Chief Priest, this form of Assembly still continued to perform relatively minor tasks such as the ratification of adoptions, installation of priests, and the making of wills. Its most significant powers, however, had already in quite early times been largely taken over by another sort of Assembly, the Comitia Centuriata, divided into *centuriae* which elected the principal annual officers of the state, normally meeting outside the Forum in the Field of Mars.[2] But by 218 BC yet another and less cumbersome form of Assembly, the Comitia Tributa, in which the citizens were grouped according to 35 territorial 'tribes', had taken over much legislation, as well as electing the tribunes who traditionally stood for the interests of the people; it also conducted certain types of trial. These meetings generally took place in the Comitium. Wooden gangways were added to the Old Rostra for elections so that voters could move up them to the dais, register their votes, and descend by the stone steps.

However, even with the tribes voting one by one, by the middle of the second century BC the little Comitium had become too small: ballots were cast in the Forum instead, on the platforms of the Temple of Castor and Pollux and the Temple of Caesar. By this time the Comitium was smaller still, being much encroached upon by buildings and monuments, and it was inevitable that its function as a meeting place for Assemblies should come to an end.

It was as part of this process that Caesar dismantled the Old Rostra in the Comitium and began to construct the new one still visible at the short end of the Forum – respectfully endowing it with the in-curved back staircase that recalled its ancient predecessor. The New Rostra at once began to witness the highest melodrama, for its platform, although still not wholly completed at the time, was apparently the place where Antony delivered his funeral speech for Julius Caesar.

Ancient opinions differed as to whether Antony's speech was really the inflammatory masterpiece given eternal renown by Shakespeare. According to the biographer Suetonius, Antony simply enumerated the honours that Caesar had received, adding a few words of his own; and a historian, Appian, agreed that Antony had spoken in brief and conciliatory terms. But another writer, Dio Cassius, believed he had made a much longer and more inflammatory speech. The biographer Plutarch knew a similar tradition, and it was Plutarch who was followed by Shakespeare.

After Caesar's body had been brought to the Forum, Antony pronounced the customary eulogy, and when he saw that the multitude was moved by his words, changed his tone to one of compassion, and taking the robe of Caesar, all bloody as it was, unfolded it to view, pointing out the many places in which it had been pierced and Caesar wounded. All further orderly procedure was at an end, of course.[3]

And so the crowd surged round and cremated Caesar's body just across the Forum, on the platform subsequently incorporated in his temple (p. 93).

Later, Antony invested the New Rostra with a further lurid distinction, for it was on its walls that he and his fellow-triumvirs, Octavian and Lepidus, displayed the lists of those who had been proscribed and sentenced to death. One of them was Cicero, and after his execution it was here that his severed head and right hand were exposed to public view. Antony, it was said, roared with laughter when they were first shown to him, and people declared that his wife Fulvia, who had previously been married to Cicero's arch-enemy Clodius, spat in the face of the dead orator and pierced his tongue with a hair-pin.

Caesar, Antony and the emperors who followed were all agreed that the Assemblies of the People should not retain any shadow of power or even nuisance value. Yet they could still be exploited for spectacular imperial purposes, being summoned, for example, for Augustus' ceremonial adoption of Tiberius as his son.[4] The main use of the New Rostra was for magnificent solemnities of this kind. For example, when Augustus died, an oration in his honour was delivered from this platform by the younger Drusus, son of the new emperor Tiberius who had already addressed the people from the Temple of Caesar where the body was lying in state.

Nero also held a particularly splendid ceremony on the New Rostra, in honour of a visiting king of Armenia, Tiridates.[5] Two years later, when Nero's downfall and death were at hand, he imagined that he might again go into the Forum and mount the Rostra and beg the people to forgive him or at least send him into honourable retirement. And after he was dead, his supporters secretly, at night, adorned the Rostra with images of him, and the texts of his decrees.

The sort of occasion which the emperors liked to stage at the place is also illustrated by two sculptured reliefs found a few yards away and now lodged in the Senate-house. They were once thought to belong to a separate Tribunal of Trajan, and they are generally known as Trajan's Plutei (balustrades) or Anaglypha (bas-reliefs); but it has instead been suggested, with a good deal of probability, that they formed the balustrades surrounding the platform of the New Rostra. One of them shows an emperor, who is, in fact, probably Trajan's successor Hadrian (AD 117–38),

addressing the people from this platform. In front of him is a seated statue of Trajan, to whom a woman, perhaps Italia, presents two children, one in her arms and one led by the hand. The panel refers to Trajan's endowment schemes for poor children, which Hadrian evidently extended. The other relief shows Hadrian standing on the dais while men bring him a heap of tablets, which he is giving the order to burn. The allusion is to his annulment of fifteen years' accumulation of debts to the state, amounting to 900 million sesterces, which was perhaps the rough equivalent of 45 million pounds – an event also commemorated by his coins (AD 118).

Both pieces of sculpture show backgrounds including interesting sketches of buildings in the Forum. They also depict a sacred fig-tree which had been miraculously transferred to a site nearby, where it grew, as its successor grows today, alongside an olive and a vine. Next to the tree is to be seen, on each of the

reliefs, a statue of the mythical Marsyas, which stood in ancient times beside the fig, olive and vine. He is best known as the musician who came to a bad end because he unwisely competed with Apollo, but here the reference is to a different thread in the tradition, according to which his name also stood for the free-

Detail of relief on p. 115; Italia presents a child to Trajan.
In the background is probably the Basilica Aemilia.
*Opposite:* Statue of Marsyas (carrying a wineskin and
standing beneath a fig tree) which symbolizes the freedom
of the citizens of Rome.

*Opposite :* Detail of relief below: Hadrian (AD 117–38) on the 'New' Rostra, presiding over Trajan's scheme for orphan children (Plutei or Anaglypha Trajani). The buildings in the background are probably the Arch of Augustus and the Temple of Castor and Pollux.

*Below :* The Plutei (or Anaglypha) of Trajan (possibly the balustrade of the 'New' Rostra); now in the Senate-house.

*Bottom :* Imaginative reconstruction of one of the scenes depicted on the Plutei (or Anaglypha) Trajani, in which Hadrian orders the burning of public debts before the Rostra. The statue of Marsyas is on the left.

*Opposite:* A bull, one of three sacrificial animals
on the Plutei (or Anaglypha) Trajani, possibly once part of
the 'New' Rostra, now standing in the Senate-house.
*Below:* Another of the sacrificial animals on the same frieze.

dom of Roman citizen communities, and the jurisdiction that guaranteed it[6]. The statue in the Forum, which has vanished, may have been brought to Rome from Apamea (Dinar) in Asia Minor in 188 BC, having been appropriated under the pretext that the town had a legendary link with Rome's ancestor Aeneas. In a regrettable nocturnal incident under Augustus, the image of Marsyas was hilariously crowned with garlands by the emperor's daughter Julia after a party.

On the opposite side of both panels there are fine representations of the three animals which were sacrificed on public ritual occasions. These include a pig, a sheep and a bull – a farmer's most valuable property, and the joint components of a traditional offering to the god Mars, dating from the primitive times when he had been an agricultural as well as a martial deity. Nearby, in the Colosseum, a Greek sorcerer was found offering up a bull with pagan ritual as late as 1522.

Reconstruction of the Curia or Senate-house showing
the vanished portico, marble facing and ornamented gable.
*Opposite:* The Senate-house building, dating from
the third century AD, has survived remarkably well.

## THE SENATE-HOUSE

NEXT to the Old Rostra, before Caesar moved it bodily
to the new site, stood the Senate-house (Curia) of
Rome. The Senate and People of the ancient formula
S.P.Q.R. had met close beside one another, and although the Senate was always the more powerful it
was tactfully forbidden to meet while the 'sovereign'
People was assembled. The last ancient reconstruction
of the Senate-house, dating from the joint reign of
Diocletian and Maximian (284–305), has survived in
remarkable condition, and now, after restoration work
in 1931–7, it can be seen in something like its original
appearance. It is true that its small portico facing the
Forum (visible in Renaissance illustrations) has gone,
and so has the marble that covered the lower part of
the brick frontage. But otherwise the exterior is intact.
A gable of the traditional pediment form is still there,
with simple ornamentation. Yet beneath it is a facade
of late Roman type, quite alien to the antique Graeco-
Roman custom. For it contains no great row of columns but consists of a plain wall only interrupted by
three large, rectangular windows with slightly
rounded tops. The bronze doors at the entrance are
copies of the originals, which were removed in the
seventeenth century to the portals of the Basilica of S.
John Lateran, where they are still to be seen today.

The interior of the Senate-house, 150 feet long and
60 feet wide, is a lofty, austere, box-like simplification,
a building reduced to an uncluttered shell of broad
planes, varied only by niches framed by small alabaster
columns. The design shows how far architecture of
the later Empire had moved away from the classical
conceptions reflected in all the temples round about.

Along either side of the interior runs a low, wide
flight of three marble-faced steps; when the Senate
voted, the noes and ayes divided to left and right. The
lowest step is wider than the others, to give room for
wooden chairs. At the far end is a dais on which the
presiding official and other functionaries had their
seats. But the most impressive feature of the interior
today is its splendid pavement of coloured marbles
inlaid in large tiles of symmetrical, ornamental patterns
which foreshadow the tiles of Byzantine and Ottoman
Constantinople.

Attached to this large council chamber were various
other structures, which have now vanished. One of
these was the Graecostasis or Station for the Greeks, an
open platform in front of the Senate-house, intended

*Opposite:* The original bronze doors of the Senate-house, now in the Basilica of St John Lateran. The Senate-house is fitted with exact copies.

*Above:* The Senate-house in 1575, an etching by Etienne Du Pérac (*Vestigi dell' Antichità di Roma*). At that time the deeply buried Senate-house possessed a bell tower and was entered by a flight of steps leading down instead of up. Metropolitan Museum of Art, New York.

for the accommodation of allied and foreign ambassadors. They could not attend the Senate's meetings, since the only non-members allowed in were sons and grandsons of Roman senators. But since the doors were left open during debates, the envoys could listen to the deliberations from this position outside. On the Graecostasis stood a small bronze shrine dedicated to Concordia – a reminder to the foreign states to behave themselves. The platform had another use also; for every day a member of the consuls' staff stood on the steps of the Senate-house, and when he saw the sun between the Old Rostra and the Graecostasis, he proclaimed that noon had arrived.[7]

Another building attached to the Senate-house (NW, according to the antiquarian Varro) was the Senaculum or Little Senate, which was a sort of antechamber used for unofficial meetings. In early times, it served as a place where senators might confer with the tribunes, who were not, originally, allowed into the Senate-house itself. Both the Graecostasis and the Senaculum were already demolished before the end of antiquity, when the sites were needed for other buildings.

To the left of the Senate-house stood the chamber which housed the senatorial archives, the Secretarium Senatus, now covered by the Via della Curia and the Church of Saint Luke and Saint Martina. The lower storey of the church still contains columns that seem to originate from the ancient building.

A further part of the complex was a courtyard known as the Chalcidicum,[8] a term used for the side rooms of large halls. Built by Augustus, this court was renamed by Domitian the Hall of Minerva, his favourite goddess. The rooms opening out upon it were employed to house documents, including records of the honourable dismissal of legionaries. The location of the courtyard is not quite certain, but Renaissance drawings suggest that it should perhaps be identified with a partially marble-paved, colonnaded, open space that can still be traced behind the Senate-house, and was formerly reached through two doors in the rear of that building. The remains of the courtyard can now be visited by passing round the Senate-house outside.

The original Senate-house, of which nothing survives, was known as the Curia Hostilia. The name was no doubt taken from the family which built it. The ancients believed it meant that the founder was the semi-legendary King Tullus Hostilius (672–640 BC). Whether this was so is unknown: but it is certain that there was already a Senate to advise the early kings. Its original membership was believed to total 100, but later the number was trebled. The Senate could meet at other public consecrated places in Rome or within one mile of the city. But its usual meeting place was this building, which consequently became the scene of a very large proportion of all the major decisions which made Rome a great power. In particular, during the early days of the Republic, the Senate showed extraordinary diplomacy in the successful reconciliation of its difficulties with the populace, that strife of oligarchs against democrats that had ruined so many Greek States. While officials came and went, as H.H. Scullard observes, 'the Senate remained. The need of a permanent governing body which could make quick decisions in times of crises led to an immense increase in its powers. Theoretically it could not legislate, but its resolutions were generally obeyed, and it came to wield a predominating moral guidance in the state.'

Tributes to the glory, grandeur and power of the Senate abound in the patriotic pages of Rome's historians. When the Gauls plundered Rome in c. 390 BC, it was said that they found those senators who were too old to bear arms seated like gods upon their chairs, awaiting their fate in serene dignity. This is only one of many allusions, throughout the centuries, to the awe which the Senate inspired in non-Roman as well as in Roman hearts. The Greeks, too, were profoundly impressed, as well they might be, since their own volatile councils, though more intellectual, made much less sense. The Thessalian diplomat, Cineas, reported to his master, king Pyrrhus of Epirus, that the Roman Senate was an assembly of kings. Subsequently its successful direction of the Punic Wars set the crown upon its fame and authority, and it was fitting that a wall of the Curia Hostilia displayed a painting of a victory over the Carthaginians and Syracusans (262

*Roman Senators Going to the Forum*; an oil painting by Jean Lemaire (1598–1659). Montreal Museum of Fine Arts.

BC). The Senate was also proud, sometimes though by no means always justifiably, of its vigilance in favour of Rome's subjects: Cicero described it as 'the greatest protection of all nations'.[9]

After various reconstructions the building was re-designed and probably enlarged by Sulla (d. 78 BC), who doubled the number of senators. No official record of senatorial proceedings was published until 59 BC, when Caesar, as consul, arranged for its regular publication, so that the people of Rome could read the foolish speeches his conservative opponents had made.

The senators wore tunics with a broad purple stripe and red leather shoes. Meetings could last from dawn until sunset, and often did. During the late Republic it was the practice of the leader of the Senate, who was usually one of the consuls, to lay the business of the day before his fellow-members, and ask them what action they desired. First he put the question to the consuls elect, and then to the exalted inner group of former consuls on whom the conduct of policy greatly depended. By Cicero's time, members had formed the custom of leaving their places and moving over to sit with the speakers they supported, whether these were ex-consuls or not.

In 52 BC, to Cicero's frequently and brilliantly ex-pressed horror, the building was burnt down in the riots attending the cremation of Clodius (52). It was restored by Sulla's son, Faustus. Soon afterwards, however, Caesar, when he redesigned the Roman Forum, began to rebuild the Senate-house once again, departing from the old, cardinal orientation and re-naming the building the Curia Julia. He had raised the membership from 600 to 900, in order to reward his partisans and bring in municipal talent; though he must have relied on many of the latter staying away, since not more than 300 members, at most, could have fitted into the hall. As was the case with many of his projects, completion and dedication had to wait for Augustus, who reduced the number of senators to the former figure of 600.

From his time onwards the Senate changed its character completely; and the change produced har-rowing experiences. There was always an emperor now, and even if he wanted the senators to be rela-tively independent – as was never quite certain – they found it difficult to estimate how far they could go. The resultant embarrassments and humiliations that were suffered in this building form one of the principal subjects of the historian Tacitus. The leading note is struck immediately, on the death of Augustus. 'They

must show neither satisfaction at the death of one em-peror, nor gloom at the accession of another: so their features were carefully arranged in a blend of tears and smiles, mourning and flattery.'[10] And it was a particu-larly exacting development that the Senate, while losing its political importance, was given new functions as a High Court – where its own members often came up for trial.

At the height of these perilous times, the emperor Domitian (81–96), though savagely suspicious and repressive towards individual senators, initiated a further reconstruction of the Senate-house, which had been burnt down under his predecessor Titus. Two centuries later it was rebuilt yet again by Diocletian and Maximian. In their day the emperor had become such an exalted, authoritarian potentate that senators had to watch their step even more carefully – and they were excluded from most of the best jobs. Yet they became socially even smarter than before, comprising, almost as a hereditary right, the best families of the empire, many of them enormously rich. Theirs is the building that we see today, as it was reconstructed after the great fire of AD 283. The pedestal of a column that still survives nearby, showing a processional scene, formed part of a five-columned monument commemorating the tenth anniversary of Diocletian's reign.

Against the far wall of the interior there are the re-mains of a pedestal, which seems to have been the base of a famous golden or gilt-bronze statue of Victory presented to the Senate-house by Augustus. Probably it had formed part of the spoils brought to Rome from the great south Italian city of Tarentum (Taras), when this was recaptured from the Carthaginians during the Second Punic War (209 BC). The statue was associated with an altar, likewise dedicated to Victory, to which senators by ancient custom paid their respects. In the fourth century AD, after Constantine had made Christianity the official religion of the Empire, pagan-ism still remained strong among the Roman upper classes; and the altar and statue became objects of the highest political significance and tension. When Constantine's son, Constantius II, paid the one visit of his long reign to Rome (AD 357), anti-pagan measures were feared. But the ancient capital made a profound impression on the emperor. He delivered a speech in the Senate-house, and the contemporary historian Ammianus writes that 'as he beheld with calm counte-nance the dutiful attendance of the Senate and the

Base of an honorary column showing a sacrifice
to Mars; part of a monument celebrating Diocletian and his
colleagues (*c.* AD 303).

august likenesses of the patrician stock, he thought, not, like Cineas, that a throng of kings was assembled together, but that the sanctuary of the whole world was present before him'.[11] However, Constantius' veneration of the Senate was not great enough to prevent him from ordering that its heathen altar of Victory should be removed.

Presumably his 'apostate' successor, Julian (361–3), restored it to its place. But in 382 the Christian ruler Gratian, when he withdrew the funds that had been used for the maintenance of the pagan cults, expelled the altar from the Senate-house again, refusing, under pressure from St Ambrose, even to receive a delegation of senators who had been dispatched to protest against these measures. After Gratian's death the supporters of the traditional religion felt they could re-open the question, and a historic debate took place in front of the young emperor Valentinian II. The leading pagan senator Symmachus spoke up for the ancient tradition. But in spite of his eloquence Ambrose ensured that the petition should once more be rejected.

However, the end had not yet come. For in the years 392–5 the imperial purple was worn by a professor named Eugenius, who, although nominally a Christian, sympathized with the pagan cause; and the altar must have been one of its institutions which he restored.[12] Eugenius did not last long, for Theodosius I suppressed him and re-established official Christianity. But writings of the time[13] suggest that the altar remained undisturbed until c. 407–10, when an intensified campaign against pagans probably resulted in its final ejection. Even then, however, the figure of Victory continued to be engraved on the coins of the Roman state. Such representations were repeated again and again until the very last emperor of the west had come and gone (476); and even thereafter Victory still appeared at Constantinople for many years to come. But in these Christian epochs she had come to symbolize the ancient greatness of Rome and no longer its old religion, for there was never again a pagan emperor, or even (as far as we know) a pagan sympathizer on the imperial throne.

The Prison (Tullianum, Carcer Mamertinus); lower cell.

# 7. Vaults and Arcades

## THE ANCIENT DUNGEONS

Owing to their discovery of concrete, the Romans built mighty vaults, round arches, and spectacular arcades which would have been inconceivable to the Greeks. The progress in these exciting techniques can be seen in the area of the Forum, from simple beginnings in the prison (Tullianum) to the massive open arches of the Record Office (Tabularium), and then by way of the fragmentary Basilica Aemilia and Basilica Julia to the superb, soaring nave and aisles of the Basilica Nova of Maxentius.

The prison of antique Rome, standing beneath the Capitol at the point where Silversmiths' Rise left the Forum area towards the north, is now completely concealed from above and outside by the church of St Joseph or San Giuseppe dei Falegnami (1598). Beneath the crypt of the church (the Cappella del Crocifisso, containing a crucifix found in the Forum) are two small ancient cells, one on top of the other. The upper cell, which was originally one of a number, possesses a rounded vault of the tunnel or barrel variety, constructed with the help of concrete. The far end of the chamber is walled in by the rock of the Capitoline Hill, and at the side runs a transverse wall cutting into the vault. The lower cell was originally circular but has again been abbreviated by another straight wall, this time at what is now the front of the building, on Silversmiths' Rise. Three rows of massive blocks of the original circumference survive. Neatly fitted without mortar, the blocks are arranged in circles which gradually narrow as the wall becomes higher. Originally it ascended to a truncated cone roofed by wooden beams, the holes for which can still be seen.[1] This lower cell is now only six and a half feet high, but the historian Sallust gave it a height of twelve feet; if he

was right, the discrepancy can be accounted for by a subsequent raising of the floor level, under which the three lowest rows of blocks may be hidden (the present floor dates from 1665).

These structures can be approximately dated by their building materials. The brown Monte Verde and Anio volcanic stones of the upper chamber[2] belong to the late second or early first century BC. The straight wall of the lower cell is made of earlier stone from Grotta Oscura of the fourth or more probably third century BC, and the circular wall of the harder, dark grey Alban stone or *peperino* which was coming into use by 250 BC. At some later stage, perhaps in the early empire, the present horizontal ceiling of this lower chamber was built. The travertine of the external wall, visible beside the present staircase descending to the prison from the street, is dated by an inscription on its lintel to a year between AD 24 and 42.

The ancient name 'Tullianum' belonged more particularly to the lower cell, and although the ancients believed it meant the chamber had been constructed by King Servius Tullius (578–534 BC), the designation may instead have come from a word meaning 'well', indicating that this was the original function of the building. This derivation is disputed; there is, however, still reported to be a small spring, and an ancient opening leads to a channel connecting with the Great Drain.

In historic times both storeys were used as Rome's prison. Although there were further dungeons in the adjacent stone-quarries *(lautumiae)* – from which the site of the Tullianum had originally been excavated – the total gaol space at Rome was evidently very limited. The early city could afford to have a small prison, not so much, as Juvenal claims, owing to the excellence of behaviour in those distant days, but because imprisonment was not a punishment in Roman law. When Caesar hoped to prevent the Senate from passing a death sentence on Catiline's fellow-conspirators in 63 BC, and instead proposed life imprisonment round the cities of Italy, the one penalty seemed as illegal as the other. Caesar added, however, that to his mind life imprisonment was worse than death.

The upper rooms were used for the detention of wrongdoers or suspects until their sentence was pronounced. The playwright Naevius, held there for libelling the noble family of the Metelli (206 BC),[3] was able to employ his detention in writing two plays which apologised for his offence. So conditions cannot have been intolerably bad on this upper floor.

The lower cell was a very different matter. It was utilised for the temporary accommodation of those condemned criminals whose execution was to take place in private rather than in public. They were let down into this dark pit to wait their end by strangling or starvation, the channel to the Great Drain being intended to eliminate not only the overflow of water from the well, but the corpses of the victims too.

The place is enclosed on all sides by walls, and above it is a chamber with a vaulted roof of stone. Neglect, darkness and stench make it hideous and fearsome to behold.[4]

It was here that Catiline's five leading fellow-conspirators were taken to be throttled. Often, however, the victims were Rome's defeated foreign enemies, led off to die here after gracing, as far as this point, the Triumphs of their conquerors, who then proceeded on their way up to the Temple of Jupiter on the Capitol. Jugurtha, king of Numidia in north Africa and Rome's inveterate enemy, and Vercingetorix who had tried to free Gaul from Julius Caesar, both died in horrible conditions in the Tullianum.

In medieval times this place was immensely venerated, as indeed it still is, because of the belief that in Nero's reign St Peter and St Paul were imprisoned here, and that they miraculously called forth the spring from the ground in order to baptise forty-nine persons, including their two gaolers, who were subsequently martyred like themselves. In the fifteenth century the Tullianum was renamed San Pietro in Carcere. When Charles Dickens was in Rome, he found that the sinister atmosphere of the cell had been enhanced by the curious custom of hanging the instruments of violent crimes upon its wall.

## THE RECORD OFFICE

Behind the prison, a towering backcloth for the whole Forum area is provided by the medieval and Renaissance Palace of the Senator (Palazzo del Senatore or Senatorio). Its front forms the centre of Michelangelo's square at the top of the Capitoline Hill (Piazza del Campidoglio), but its back, reaching down to a much lower level, looks over the Forum. As seen today from the Forum side, the building is flanked on the left by a partly visible, fifteenth-century tower and on the right by a great crenellated buttress. Between them are the two top storeys (and a small one above) of the Palace of the Senator, dating in its present form from 1582–1605. But below these storeys, still on the Forum side, is to be seen one of the most important buildings of the ancient city, the Record Office or National Archives (Tabularium).

These remains are very extensive, and are much more substantial than any others of Republican date in all Rome. As S. B. Platner declared, 'this is by far the most interesting, as well as the best preserved, specimen of Republican architecture'. Its appearance today, in combination with the un-antique palace rising above, symbolizes the position of this vast edifice as the boundary between the Capitol and the Forum – between living and ruined Rome.

This surviving external wall of the ancient Record Office, looking down upon the Forum, was once covered by stucco. Now that covering has gone, and what remains is the masonry beneath, consisting of a huge mass of rectangular stone blocks eleven feet thick. The lower part of the ancient wall comprises a thirty-six foot high substructure, the sort of base that is characteristic of ancient Italian building. It is lodged in the flank of the Capitoline Hill, and masks the dip between its two summits – the citadel and Jupiter's temple. Within this substructure, at a point where a row of tall narrow windows can be seen today, there is a concealed corridor between hill and outer wall.

The Temple of Romulus on the Sacred Way; the bronze doors and lock are original.

*Overleaf:* View across the Forum to the Arch of Septimius Severus and the Record Office (Tabularium).

The Record Office (Tabularium); above it the Palace of
the Senator; the earliest visible parts are fifteenth century.
*Opposite:* In the Basilica Julia; the Church of Santa Maria
in Cannapara.

Above the substructure, between it and the lowest visible level of the Palace of the Senator, is a further antique storey, which appears today as a wall interrupted by huge round arches $24\frac{1}{2}$ feet high and 12 feet wide, each flanked by engaged Doric columns and topped by a horizontal lintel.[5] These arches are now only three in number, but seven others which originally existed were filled in with brick during the Middle Ages. For a long time only one of the arches was open, but two more have been cleared in recent years. It has not proved possible to uncover any others because the building above is so heavy; and the ancient stone has been greatly corroded by salt, which was stored here in the Middle Ages.

Originally, then, this was a most imposing arcade of ten enormous arches. Behind the arches runs a great gallery, which nowadays looks out over the Forum from the three apertures, but was once completely open. On top of this gallery stood another, which was demolished in the sixteenth century to make way for the rebuilding of the Palace of the Senator. Probably the arcade of this upper gallery consisted, in its original form, of Ionic columns, replaced by Corinthian in a reconstruction by Vespasian.

Behind these galleries were vaulted rooms, partially cut into the rock and grouped in a rectangle round a large central court.[6] On the surviving storey, there are still extensive remains of these rooms, and something can be seen of them from the gallery. A further view is available, if the porter will let one have a look, from the door on the left-hand side of the Capitoline facade of the Palace of the Senator. 'Particularly at night,' as Georgina Masson says, 'when the lights concealed by great terracotta urns illuminate the vaults, this is an extraordinarily evocative sight, and one has the eerie sensation of looking into a passage that leads backwards into the very heart of time.'

As an inscription inside the building indicates, the Record Office was finished and dedicated by the respected conservative leader Catulus, consul in 78 BC. But it had been planned by his friend Sulla, who died in this year after reigning as dictator from 81 until his abdication in 79. The dominating mass of the Record Office is Sulla's most conspicuous surviving memorial. The rest of his bold town-planning was swept away and lost sight of. But beneath the surface much of the present layout of the area is due to him. For after a fire in the civil wars which had destroyed the Capitoline temple, he took the opportunity to re-design most of the Forum, laying down new and improved pavements and moving the orientation away from the cardinal points of the compass, as well as abolishing, adding, and altering many minor monuments.

He also introduced or developed important architectural innovations. In particular, the arches of the first-storey arcade of the Record Office were of great significance to the future because they combined the traditional, Greek columnar post-and-lintel, vertical and horizontal, type of architecture with the new Roman round arch. These arches are now found framed within the columns and their horizontal lintel: the curve is set within straight lines, the circle within the square.

Round arches were nothing new, but hitherto their history had not been by any means so spectacular. They had been attempted sparingly by the Egyptians and Assyrians. The recent discovery at Elea (Velia), in Greek south Italy, of a twelve-foot-high gateway dating from the fourth century BC indicates that the form was not as wholly unfamiliar to the Greeks as had previously been believed. At Volaterrae (Volterra) in Etruria, a relief of the third century BC seems to show that the round arch of the city-gate called the Porta all'Arco was already in existence at that time. The Etruscans also used circular arches for drains and culverts, and there are small early arches in the Forum[7] which were designed to cover tributaries of the Great Drain or the channels which drained the blood from altars. The sixteen-foot-high arch of the Drain itself where it debouches in the Tiber dates from before 100 BC; and as we shall see, simple free-standing arches gradually evolved from the same period onwards (Chapter 8).

But here in the Record Office we have the immensely fruitful and typically Roman formula of whole rows of arches, set in arcades that were designed on a grand scale and superimposed one upon another (though the top arcade has now disappeared). This formula, as later elaborated in the Colosseum beyond the other end of the Forum, was destined to produce many Renaissance masterpieces, notably Michelangelo's palaces on the other side of the Record Office, upon the Capitoline Hill.

Inside the Record Office (Tabularium); the great gallery which looks out over the Forum from its three remaining arched apertures once contained ten open arches.

We cannot tell where or when this idea came into being. It may have been one of the novel architectural conceptions which Sulla brought back from his campaigning in the east. In any case, here at the Record Office, it was already being handled with bold confidence. The exploitation of such forms was greatly facilitated by the innovation of concrete, which had graduated from substructures and unambitious vaults, like those of the prison described in the last section, and was now being employed to take the thrustless weight of huge arches.

The engaged columns of the Record Office's arcade were merely the frames of these arches, and no longer served the structural purpose for which columns had originally been designed by the Greeks. For now, even if they added a certain strength, they are little more than surface decorations upon the mighty concrete-covered pylons or piers flanking the arches.

As for the piers, they are the front ends of partitions that reach back over the gallery and divide it into compartments or bays. The ceilings of these bays are not flat, wooden affairs but solid vaults displaying a number of different forms. This too was made possible by concrete. In a building for the national archives, it was a vital consideration to avoid the inflammable material of wood. The same requirement dictated the use, for the outer walls, of stone from Gabii which, although too flaky to be a good background for stucco, was particularly impervious to fire.[8]

The varying kinds of vault in the Record Office provided important legacies to Europe. The compartments in the front gallery, each measuring fifteen by sixteen feet, had concrete roofs consisting of an unusual, slightly flattened kind of cross (groin) vaulting, produced by the right-angled intersection of a pair of ordinary semicircular tunnel or barrel vaults. At the back, one chamber on the north side seems to have possessed a more elaborate cross vault, while other rooms (if one could see them) show the plain tunnel vaults already found in the prison.

The Record Office was probably intended to serve not only as a storage place for archives but as an annexe and partial replacement of the national Treasury in the Temple of Saturn, which lay beneath its towering facade on the Forum side. Considering the importance of this Office, it is mentioned surprisingly little in ancient literature. But there is a probable reference in Virgil, who speaks of the happy farmer caring nothing for the metal tablets of the law, and for the lunatic Forum, and for the Record Office *(tabularia)* of the people.[9]

The two ground-levels at the opposite sides of the building, Forum below and Capitol and central courtyard above, were linked together by an internal flight of 66 steps. Parts of this staircase, roofed with stepped sections of concrete tunnel vaulting, are still excellently preserved, although its large entrance-door on the Forum side has been closed up. This was probably done when the Temple of Vespasian was being built between the Record Office and the Forum; the Temple also did a lot to spoil the view of the Office from this side. When Vespasian's adherents prematurely occupied the Capitol during the Civil Wars of AD 69, the staircase may have provided one of the routes by which the supporters of his enemy Vitellius launched a counter-attack.[10] The result of the fighting was that the Temple of Jupiter on the Capitol was once again burnt to the ground. Vespasian rebuilt it, and at the same time restored or reconstructed the upper arcade of the Record Office, now obliterated by the Palace of the Senator.

## THE BASILICA AEMILIA

These arches and arcades had developed from the plain colonnades – rows of columns without round arches inside them – which had played so great a part in the Greek and then Roman architecture of the previous centuries. For more than a hundred years before the Record Office, that simpler formula had been characteristic of Basilicas in Rome. These magnified and improved adaptations from Greek models were rectangular roofed halls serving as meeting-places for social and commercial activities, and for the proceedings of the law. The earliest surviving example of an Italian Basilica is at Pompeii (? *c.* 120 BC). It is a large, rectangular structure, and is now believed to have possessed a roof, a flat one; its interior was surrounded by a continuous colonnade – a temple turned inside out. The Pompeii building perhaps gives us some idea of what the earliest hall of the same type beside the Roman Forum was like. This had been the Basilica Porcia, built by Cato the Censor (184 BC)[11] just west of the Senate-house (on the site of the old stone-quarries and prison annex). The building was completely destroyed by fire during the disturbances following the brutal murder of Clodius in the Forum in 52 BC.

Fallen Corinthian columns in the Basilica Aemilia are the relics of its four great colonnades, those in the interior of black, red and white African marble and green *cipollino* from Euboea.

Then came the Basilica Aemilia (179, first called
'Fulvia et Aemilia') and the Basilica Sempronia (170,
later Julia) of which the ground plans, but unfortunately all too little else, can still be seen flanking the
Forum on each of its long sides.

The original Basilica Aemilia (NE of the Forum) was
another internally colonnaded, oblong hall. Its nave
was probably taller than the side aisles; if so, the upper
walls of the nave, rising above the aisle roofs, were lit
at this high level by rows of small windows anticipating the clerestories of Romanesque and Gothic
churches. In 159 BC the Basilica was furnished with
Rome's first reliable timepiece, a water-clock, which
was a considerable improvement on the sundials used
previously.

When the building was reconstructed just after its
centenary in 78 BC, it was given a colonnade outside
as well as in – or rather two, for one was placed on top
of the other. The coins which indicate these features
confirm that, in accordance with a custom borrowed
from the Greeks, shields were attached to the horizontal courses between the upper and lower colonnade.[13] It is also clear from the coins that the lower of
the colonnades was Doric and the upper one Corinthian; and the same sketches seem to indicate that the
short ends of the Basilica were crowned by gables or
pediments.

The coins do not, however, suggest that there were
any round arches between these external columns:
they formed colonnades, not arcades. It was evidently
when the building was again lavishly rebuilt by another member of the Aemilian family (55–34 BC), with

The Basilica Aemilia as restored by Marcus Aemilius
Lepidus (78 BC), on a silver *denarius* issued not
long afterwards.
*Right:* Reconstructions of the Basilica Aemilia: above,
first to fourth centuries; below, fifth to sixth centuries.
*Opposite:* Drawing by Giuliano da Sangallo of the
marble facade of the Basilica Aemilia in the sixteenth
century. Vatican Library.

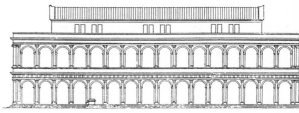

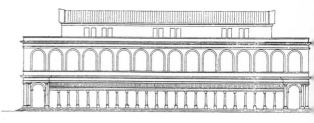

inds initially supplied as a political bribe by Julius Caesar, that the concrete-cored circular arches were dded, so as to make an enormous two-storeyed rcade backing on the Basilica's outside wall, of which good deal still survives. Henceforward, if not earlier, he New Shops were incorporated in the outer gallery etween arcade and wall. It was probably at the same me that an additional aisle or ambulatory was added o the interior on the side farthest from the Forum, ringing the building to its final dimensions of 308 by 9 feet. Corresponding to the two external storeys vere superimposed internal colonnades consisting of onic and Corinthian columns of black, red and white frican marble, and green and white *cipollino* from uboea. The ceilings were still flat and made of wood. large, two-storeyed frontal portico was erected on he short side facing the Senate-house.

After a fire of 14 BC, the Basilica Aemilia was sumptuously restored once more under Augustus, who incorporated a chapel in honour of his grandsons Gaius and Lucius beside the New Shops (SE). Another restoration was undertaken by Tiberius on the two hundredth anniversary of the Basilica. At one of these stages, the frontal portico was adorned with an elaborate frieze.

Part of the rich relief sculpture of the interior of the building, probably dating from the time of Augustus, is still to be seen on the spot, while other portions are preserved in the Forum Museum. Executed in the vigorous, plastic manner of late Greek (Hellenistic) art, it includes various scenes from Roman legend, including the story of Aeneas and his escape from Troy to be the legendary ancestor of Rome, and the rape of the Sabine women by Romulus' men.

*Opposite:* Copy of a statue from the Basilica Aemilia.
*Below:* Relief of a Maenad or dancer from the Basilica
Aemilia. Both are now in the Forum Museum.

Frieze from the Basilica Aemilia, now in the Forum
Museum; the traitress Tarpeia is overwhelmed
by enemy shields.

*Opposite:* Another frieze from the Basilica Aemilia now on
display in the Forum Museum; the rape of the Sabine women.

Decorative frieze from the Basilica Aemilia.
*Opposite:* The ruined Basilica Aemilia (originally Fulvia et Aemilia), probably destroyed by Alaric the Visigoth in AD 410.

Yet the Basilica itself is now only a gutted shell. It has become tragically hard to appreciate Pliny the elder's assertion that this was one of the three most beautiful buildings in the world.[14] Destruction by fire, to which a wooden-roofed building such as this was particularly liable, descended once again in the fifth century AD, probably when Alaric the Visigoth sacked the city in 410. On that fatal day the money changers from the New Shops, who habitually came into the Basilica to conduct their business, were carrying on as usual. But green stains which are still visible on the sumptuous pavement show the fate of their stock, since these marks are the remains of their copper coins which were fused into the marble floor by the conflagration. When, a century later, Theoderic the Ostrogoth restored a number of buildings, he seems to have regarded the Basilica Aemilia as beyond serious repair.

## THE BASILICA JULIA

On the other side of the Forum rose the not very dissimilar Basilica Julia, which Caesar began to erect on the site of the earlier Basilica Sempronia. After a fire, it was restored on an enlarged site by Augustus, who gave it the names of his grandsons Gaius and Lucius. The building suffered again in the great fire of 283, and

was reconstructed once more; and after Alaric's sack further restoration work was undertaken.

Today the Basilica Julia is as miserable a shell as its counterpart across the Forum. But its ground plan is again clearly to be seen, and this shows that it was even larger than the Aemilian building; it measures 315 by 158 feet. Like the Basilica Aemilia, it confronted the Forum with a two-storeyed external arcade of round arches, with their piers incorporating engaged columns. In the galleries of the arcade, which in this building opened straight into the main hall without a continuous separating wall, there were again shops – the successors of the Old Shops which had stood here in humble independence before these vast buildings existed. Inside, the Basilica Julia possessed two internal aisles round all four sides, with their circular arches decorated with sculptured heads on the keystones and supported by piers incorporating engaged pilasters. The aisles had concrete cross-vaulted ceilings, though

their external roofs were flat. Flat, also, at a higher level, were the ceiling and the roof of the nave.

It was from these roofs that Caligula scattered gold and silver money to the people of Rome for several days in succession. Many perished in the scramble: more than three centuries later the figure was still remembered as 32 men, 247 women and a eunuch.[15] There was a rumour that the emperor had made a special contribution to these amusing casualties by throwing down pieces of iron as well as coins. This same flat roof of the Basilica Julia formed a stage in a shortlived bridge that Caligula built in order to link the Capitoline and Palatine hills: the residences of Olympian Jupiter, and of the emperor who was his nearest equivalent upon earth. The total distance covered by the bridge was 820 feet, and at one point it stood 98 feet above the ground. However, it was probably not much more than a series of gangways, mainly wooden, leading from roof to roof.

From the ruined church of Santa Maria in Cannapara in the Basilica Julia.
*Left:* Reconstruction of the interior of the Basilica Julia.
*Opposite:* The inscription to Lucius Caesar from the portico of Augustus and his grandsons Gaius and Lucius, attached to the Basilica Aemilia.

The substructure beside the Palatine Hill.
*Opposite:* A reconstruction of the Basilica Julia, where
Roman justice was administered.

While the Basilica Aemilia was primarily a business centre, the Basilica Julia was above all a place of law-courts, recalling that one of the most important functions of the Forum, with which indeed its name became synonymous, was the provision of the famous Roman justice – 'the Forum', as Cicero called it, 'in which all justice is preserved'. Hitherto a large part of this majestic process had been housed in more or less temporary tribunals, in various parts of the Forum. Caesar built the Basilica Julia with the intention of bringing together some of these various courts; though, in fact, litigation continued to proliferate, and so did the places where it was conducted.

Under the empire the Basilica Julia housed the board of the Centumviri who dealt with civil suits. They numbered at this time not a hundred members, as their name would suggest, but a hundred and eighty.

whole racket, winning applause from the other three tribunals as well as his own.[16]

Some speakers employed gangs of professional applauders, or 'supper-praisers' as the Romans called them. Their activities added further to the deafening hubbub; but signs of enthusiasm of this kind were deemed necessary to palliate the boredom of speeches, since these were frequently very long. An effort was made to restrict their length by the use of public water-clocks, which had replaced sundials for the measurement of time. A speaker was allowed only a certain number of clocks. But we learn with dismay that Pliny the younger was on one occasion permitted sixteen clocks – adjusted, by special authorization, to run slowly – which enabled him to speak for over five hours.[17] Diagrams scratched on the floor of the Basilica, mostly circular but some rectangular, served

These judges performed their duties sitting either in two or four panels, separated only by curtains and screens. Crowds were enormous, and the acoustics, at least in the upper galleries, proved imperfect; but Quintilian, in the later first century AD, recalled one speaker, the former consul Publius Galerius Trachalus, whose voice was powerful enough to drown the

as boards on which visitors passed the time playing games. They recall Cicero's reference to a 'rascal not ashamed to play dice even in the Forum'.

Caesar created a precedent by building a new Forum of his own outside the Roman Forum – the first of the huge imperial Fora which drained a proportion of the crowds away from the old town centre.

Yet his contribution to the old Roman Forum, too, by constructing or reconstructing the splendid arcaded fronts of the Basilicas Aemilia and Julia, was as great as that of his predecessor Sulla, or even greater. When the Forum was sealed on its fourth and last side, soon afterwards, by the temple erected in his memory, it became an enclosed piazza and almost a closed interior, shut in at this final end by the temple's new facade and on every other side by a great two-storeyed rhythm of columns, arches and arcades.

The effect was further enhanced by the presence of other arcaded structures to the south-east of the open space. At this point, beyond the New Way, there are still enormous remains of massive superimposed arches. At least four storeys of projecting arcades masked the steep slope of the Palatine Hill, prolonging outwards the foundations of the imperial palaces above. Furthermore, the whole hill was again enlarged, in this same direction of the Forum, by two further buildings erected against its slope. One is the tripartite edifice which subsequently became the Church of Santa Maria Antiqua; originally it seems to have been the guard house of Domitian's palace on the Palatine.

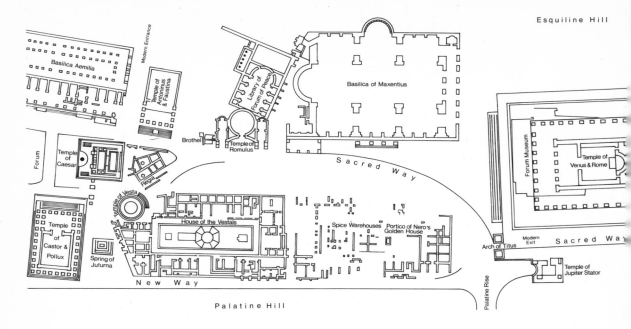

Esquiline Hill

Basilica Aemilia

Modern Entrance

Temple of Antoninus & Faustina

Library of Forum of Peace

Basilica of Maxentius

Forum Museum

Temple of Venus & Rome

Brothel

Temple of Romulus

Temple of Caesar

Forum

Regia

S a c r e d   W a y

Temple of Vesta

House of the Vestals

Spice Warehouses

Portico of Nero's Golden House

Temple of Castor & Pollux

Arch of Titus

Modern Exit

S a c r e d   W a y

Spring of Juturna

Palatine Rise

Temple of Jupiter Stator

N e w   W a y

Palatine Hill

Plan of the south-east section of the Forum.
*Below:* Reconstruction of the Basilica Nova of Maxentius
and Constantine showing the original situation of the
three great arches which still stand today.

*Right:* One of the columns of the Basilica Nova of
Maxentius and Constantine which now stands
in the Piazza Santa Maria Maggiore, crowned with a
statue of the Madonna and Child.

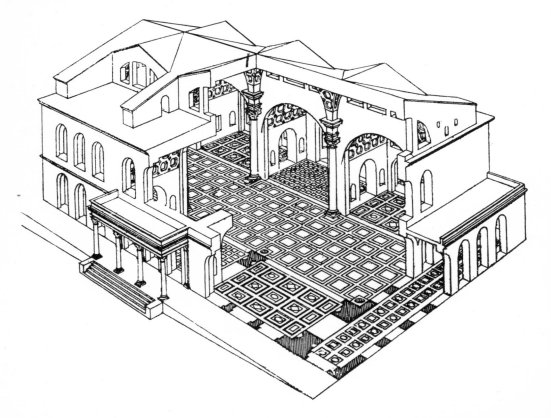

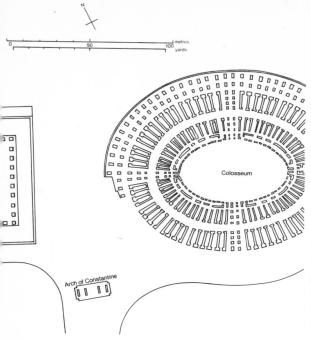

It is sometimes fashionable to decry mere size, but when the scale is so vast as this, and when, as here, it is achieved by architecture of outstanding brilliance, such dimensions add a new and fresh character to a building. As Sir Mortimer Wheeler remarks, 'the crowning gift of the Roman empire to architecture was magnitude. With magnitude of course went many other qualities, but most of them were in some measure attendant upon magnitude; they were literally of epoch-making importance.'

The Basilica of Maxentius was divided, on both its long and its short axis, into a nave and two aisles: there was a long nave and a short one, each with its flanking aisles. The divisions between the naves and their aisles, out in the open hall, consisted of four huge piers – only four, compared to the seventy-four columns of the Basilica Julia which had only been one-third as large. In front of the piers stood Corinthian columns forty-seven feet high, made of a creamy,

Next to it is a niched hall, measuring 107 by 80 feet, which towers right up to the ground-level of the Palatine itself. Wrongly known as the Temple of Augustus, it apparently served the palace of Domitian as a monumental vestibule.[18] The brick underfacing, which has survived the loss of its marble cover, displays massive but confusing remnants of an elaborate, rising composition of arches and sham arches, culminating in a huge vault sixty feet above the ground. The building was buttressed on the west side by rows of shops and fronted by a columned portico.

## THE BASILICA NOVA OF MAXENTIUS: THE CLIMAX OF ROMAN ARCHITECTURE

The most magnificent monument in the whole Forum stands a little more than one hundred yards east of the Basilica Aemilia, upon the Sacred Way. It is the 'New' Basilica, known as that of Maxentius and Constantine, since it was begun by Maxentius (306–12) – the last pagan emperor to choose Rome for the capital – and completed by his victor Constantine the Great (312–37).

This gigantic edifice was a rectangle terminating at its NW and NE ends in apses, of which the latter survives. It is three hundred and fifty feet long (NW–NE) and nearly two hundred feet in width (NE–SW).

*Above:* Imaginative reconstruction of the interior of the Basilica Nova.

*Opposite:* The three great arches of the ruined Basilica Nova of Maxentius (or Constantine); a contemporary view and a sixteenth-century engraving by Hier. Cock.

red-veined marble from the Sea of Marmora. They have vanished from the site, but one, converted to a Christian purpose, can still be seen in another part of Rome, the Piazza Santa Maria Maggiore. The columns of the Basilica of Maxentius, however, did not bear the weight of the huge vaults, which were directly carried by the concrete-cored piers on which the columns were little more than decorative attachments.

And so, in spite of earthquakes and other devastations, a large part of this building, the three terminal spans (NE) of the shorter nave and aisles, continued to stand even after their columns had gone. And they still stand today: three arches of the same size, eighty feet high and sixty-seven feet across, the width of the present St Peter's (whose architects studied the building carefully)[19]. Their original tunnel-vaulting, too, can still be seen, with its sunken ornamental panels. The straight walls at the ends of the lateral aisles are broken by two rows of three great, arched windows. The nave, on the other hand, terminates in a rounded

ose, which likewise survives: it develops, on an enormous scale, the apsidal construction which had long
been a feature of Roman architecture. A comparable
piece of virtuosity in this same field, smaller though
still very large, can be seen in the twin apses, back to
back, of the Temple of Venus and Rome just beyond,
built by Hadrian and his successor but restored by
Aurelian (AD 270–5) and Maxentius.[20]

When Maxentius started the Basilica, this apse on
the shorter axis did not exist, for, according to his
version of the building, the only apse was on the
longer axis, at its north-western extremity facing the
Forum, and the only entrance consisted of a portico at
the opposite end. The long nave which extended
between this entrance and apse has not survived, but
unlike the shorter nave it was taller than its aisles,
rising to a height of no less than 115 feet, higher than
Westminster Abbey. Constantine, however, altered
his plan in c. AD 313, making the shorter axis the main
one instead. With this in mind he constructed a

VENERI·FELICI·ET·ROMAE·AETERNAE·IMP·CAES·AELIVS·HADRIANVS·EX·S·C

*Above:* Imaginative reconstruction of the exterior
of the Temple of Venus and Rome.
*Left:* Brass coin of Hadrian (*c.* AD 136), founder of the
Temple of Venus and Rome, showing the Temple.
*Opposite:* Interior of the Temple of Venus and Rome
today.

further portico on the sw side upon the Sacred Way. It was framed by porphyry columns, which partly survive, and was approached by a long flight of steps. Inside, at the far end, rose a new apse, which is the one we see today. It was set apart by a lofty columned balustrade, and apparently served to house the tribunal which, according to the tradition for Basilicas, heard legal cases in the building.

The walls were punctuated with niches. What remains today is brick-faced; originally there were marble facings up to a certain height, and above came a covering of stucco. The white stucco on the vaults was overlaid by gilding and paint, and there was sculptural decoration too, for part of a frieze of sea-gods and nymphs is preserved in the Forum Museum. The pavement was made of variegated marbles, red, green, yellow and white.

Hitherto the elevated naves of Basilicas had possessed windowed walls extending beside and above the roofs of their lateral aisles; and sometimes, though not here in the Roman Forum, they had terminated in apses. The longer nave of the Basilica of Maxentius repeated both these features, but they were transformed not only in scale but in the manner of their application. For one thing, the roof was not flat but vaulted, in massive extension of the principles seen at work in the Record Office. The Basilica of Maxentius is less comparable with the Aemilian or Julian Basilicas, which had flat roofs, than with the vaulted palace halls that the empire's eastern neighbours and enemies, the Parthians, had put up at Hatra and Asshur near the Tigris, or the enormous arched, side-chapelled throne room that their successors, the Persians, had erected late in the previous century at their capital Ctesiphon on the same river.

And yet the basic concept of the Basilica of Maxentius was Roman, for it was founded on Roman models: not, as has been said, on the Basilicas that had been seen hitherto, but on the halls of the Palatine palaces, and above all on the huge central halls that formed the divisions of Roman Baths. What had been done here was to plan a structure of the same kind but to design it in detached isolation as a separate building. It was in the great halls of the Baths that such vaults and semi-domes and apses, based on the gradually improving technique of lightweight, thrustless concrete, had been given increasingly powerful expression, until they became the most characteristic and pre-eminent achievement of Roman architecture. All the features

of earlier Baths had been incorporated, with added grandeur, in the Baths of Caracalla which were built in south-eastern Rome during the early third century AD. In spite of its human purposes, the scale of this architecture spoke no longer of humanism but of a new age in which the individual is a minute component of a mass. The central feature of Caracalla's complex was a cross-vaulted hall carried not on a row of columns but only on four enormous piers, as in the Basilica of Maxentius. And then the Baths which Diocletian built on the Viminal Hill, after the great fire of 283, seem to have been twice as large again. A mere half of their central hall now comprises the very big church of Santa Maria degli Angeli.

Such were the models for the New Basilica. In some respects, it is true, it differed from the halls of the Baths, for their aisles or side-chambers had been more like separate galleries or passage-ways, whereas in the Basilica they were thrown open to form integral parts of the main structure. And yet the building faithfully follows the main principle of the great Bath halls which, with their greatly reduced number of internal supports, had aimed at the maximum dematerialization of the internal space.

This principle was again embodied in the planning of the Basilica's huge rounded windows, such as can still be seen at the ends of the shorter aisles. As at Augusta Trevirorum (Trier) on the Moselle, where the same method is used in a contemporary Basilica and Baths, these windows not only introduced a novel method of lighting but created an emphatic rhythmical relation of window to wall. The walls look medieval, and the shape of the windows anticipate Romanesque, for the architects of this early fourth century AD had already far outstripped the old classical post-and-lintel procedures seen in the temples that clustered round about.

The new building, then, is a prototype of the cathedrals of the future. And it foreshadows their vaulted naves as well, for the ceilings of the Basilica of Maxentius displayed vaults both of the intersecting (cross or groin) variety, in the main long nave, and of the tunnel (barrel) type in the short nave and aisles forms that had already been tried out at the Record Office four centuries earlier. Moreover, as in certain earlier buildings, another big anti-classical step had also been taken. The columns attached to the arches were no longer surmounted by continuous horizontal blocks, those entablatures which throughout the classical age had been an obligatory accompaniment

The coffered vaults of the Basilica Nova
seen from across the Sacred Way, with medieval structures
in the foreground.

of the columnar form; for here they would only have got in the way of the great open spaces between the arches. The shorter naves and aisles show arches which exist quite independently of the columns that stood decoratively in front of their piers. But the columns served a second purpose as well, for from above their lintels soared even higher arches, now vanished, which rose to the height of the ceiling vaults of the longer, higher nave and formed an angle with them.

All this, then, seems anticipatory of the Middle Ages. Nevertheless, the process of development from Constantinian to Romanesque was not, as far as ecclesiastical buildings were concerned, continuous. For Constantine's own Christian Basilicas abandoned these lofty vaults and went back to the horizontal wooden ceilings of the Basilicas Aemilia and Julia. Such old-fashioned ceilings seemed to fit in better with the parallel, concentrated architectural movement of nave and aisles towards the eastern end which was a ritual requirement of a Christian church. It was not until seven hundred more years had passed that the architects of cathedrals began to use vaults competing in size and boldness with this masterpiece of the early fourth century AD.

When Constantine changed the shape of Maxentius' Basilica, he used the old apse, at the NW end of the longer nave, to frame a colossal seated statue of himself. Its body glittered in a robe of gilded bronze, but the metal has not survived. Nor has the core beneath it, which was made of wood, unless the interior was hollow. But the unclothed parts of the statue were marble, of which gigantic fragments are still to be seen in the courtyard of the Palazzo dei Conservatori on the Capitoline Hill. They comprise the head, the bent left knee, the two feet, and the right hand (perhaps taken over from a much earlier figure) grasping the remains of a sceptre. The head alone is nine feet high and weighs eight or nine tons. Here are the fabulous dimensions of the Basilica again, this time devoted to sculpture and to a single individual.

A silver medallion issued by Constantine at the time when he was reconstructing the building shows him wearing a helmet which bears the monogram XP, the Greek initial letters of Christ, and the same sacred

*Above and left:* Head of Constantine the Great from the Basilica Nova; now in the courtyard of the Palazzo dei Conservatori.

emblem may have been fastened to the staff in the statue's hand. For under the image, we are told, he had this inscription engraved: 'Through this sign of salvation, which is the true symbol of goodness, I rescued your city and freed it from the tyrant's yoke, and through my act of liberation I restored the Senate and People of Rome to their ancient renown and splendour.'[21]

That, however, was a somewhat ironical profession from the ruler who was about to confirm the demotion of Rome from its position as the capital city of the empire, since he established a new permanent capital far away on the shores of the Bosphorus. Moreover, it was Constantine who raised the totalitarian fourth-century State to a new pitch of ferocious severity. The emperor now possessed an unapproachable grandeur that the early empire had never known; and Constantine was enthroned here like the effigy of a god. Yet he was no god, but the vicegerent and earthly mirror of the Christian Deity – though just how Constantine conceived the new official religion is a matter of conjecture. At all events, here was the man at whose court, resplendent and hieratic like the courts of Persian monarchs, writers felt it appropriate to speak of the 'Divine Face' and 'Sacred Countenance'. The sculptor has conceived this countenance as a holy mask, an overpowering cult object resembling, though on a far greater scale, the icons of future Byzantium: an idol animated with the divine presence, and with the power to repel the demons lurking in pagan images.

# 8. The Monumental Arches

And so the formula of a novel rounded arch within the traditional classical frame was brought to perfection in a succession of mighty vaulted and arcaded buildings. But the idea could also be pursued in isolation from arcades, and even from any buildings at all. The result was that highly characteristic Roman creation, the monumental or commemorative arch, which has had a greater influence on Europe than any of Rome's other architectural gifts, with the single exception of the Colosseum.

Two superb and peculiarly influential specimens are to be seen in the neighbourhood of the Forum.

The first recorded examples of free-standing arches at Rome date from 196 BC, when one was set up in the Cattle Market (Forum Boarium) and another in the Circus Maximus south of the Palatine.[1] The latter was erected on the central barrier of the course, and not, that is to say, in a position where any processions would walk under its span. This arch cannot, therefore, have been intended for any functional purpose. It still remains possible, however, that earlier commemorative arches, now lost, may have evolved from processional origins. If so, such processions are likely to have been connected with the magic associated with gates, magic that was especially applicable to conquerors going out to war and returning from it (Appendix 2, Temple of Janus).

During the same second century BC, a period which was productive of a great deal of architectural innovation, the Romans built at least three other arches in the capital. One of them, defrayed from the spoils of a Gallic war, spanned the Sacred Way at the point where it entered the open space of the Forum. This was the Arch of Fabius or Fornix Fabianus, the word *fornix* apparently indicating that this was not a monumental arch *(arcus)* in the later sense of the word – ornamented with columns and other decoration – but a simple span with no such classical surface attached to its pylons.[2] It was not until the imperial age that the free-standing, ornamental, columnar arch became at all frequent, and even quite late in the first century AD Pliny the elder could still describe it as a modern invention.[3]

## THE ARCH OF TITUS

Pliny died in 79, the year in which the emperor Titus came to the throne. Titus himself died only two years later, and the arch devoted to his memory is one of the most pure and chaste examples of this architectural institution. It stands at the highest point of the Sacred Way, where processions could pass under it, and looks across the Forum to the temple dedicated to Titus and his father Vespasian at the other end. This arch, which is made of Attic marble from Mount Pentelicon (with nineteenth-century travertine additions), commemorated Titus' bloodthirsty conquest of the Jewish Revolt and his destruction of Jerusalem (AD 70). The arch has a single opening, flanked by pylons incorporating on each side two engaged, fluted columns of the Composite Order – a Roman mixture of Ionic and Corinthian that had perhaps been invented in the time of Augustus, with the former Order's spirals and the latter's acanthus leaves. The opening is surmounted by two horizontal storeys, the higher of which displays inscriptions, repeated on either front, indicating

The Arch of Titus, built to commemorate the sack of Jerusalem by Titus in AD 70.

that the monument was dedicated to Titus' memory by his brother and successor Domitian.[4]

The insertion of a round arch within the vertical and horizontal lines of Graeco-Roman architecture means that these lines lose their original functional purpose. And yet the formula of the monumental arch permitted the deployment of a whole panoply of classical motifs, and to the student of the 'grammar' of ancient architecture it is almost, as Sir John Summerson says, 'a grammatical treatise in itself – it gives the clue to so many possible moves in the classical game'.

The Arch of Titus is decorated by a large amount of sculpture. In ancient times there was much more, because an elaborate bronze statuary group stood on the top, displaying Vespasian and Titus in a four-horse chariot. The triangles between the curved parts of the

On the keystone of the vault of the Arch of Titus; the Emperor Titus is borne to heaven by the eagle of Jupiter.
*Right:* The Colosseum seen through the Arch of Titus.

arch and its right-angled framework are decorated with winged Victories holding standards. Above is a frieze (on rather too small a scale) which represents scenes of a Triumphal procession; a figure reclining in a litter perhaps represents the captive River Jordan. The ceiling inside the opening is vaulted with a rich offering of sunken squares and decorated with a relief of the emperor being carried to heaven by an eagle.

On either flank of this inside tunnel of the arch are reliefs representing the two principal moments of Titus' Triumph. One of them shows the Triumphal procession approaching an arch. Young men wearing laurel wreaths are carrying the spoils plundered from the Temple of Jerusalem: here, as Shelley declared, 'is sculptured, in deep relief, the desolation of a city'. The other relief shows the Goddess Rome leading the

*Below:* Rome leading the four-horse triumphal chariot of Titus.
*Opposite:* Sculpted friezes on the Arch of Titus; the Emperor Titus rides
in his triumphal car while Victory places a wreath on his head.

Triumphal four-horse chariot of Titus, while Victory, accompanied by the twin deities Honour and Courage (Virtus), places a wreath upon his head. His official attendants, the lictors, can be seen in the background.

The talented designer of these reliefs, like portrait-sculptors of this same age, emphasizes the points of highest relief by deep shadows and vivid contrasts of light and shade. As in slightly earlier mural paintings at Pompeii, which was obliterated by Mount Vesuvius in Titus' reign, there is an advance towards illusion: the illusion of movement seen through a window silhouetted against the sky. These experiments fall short of complete realism, but display realistic effects that are not unconvincing. The cleverly superimposed planes give an impression of depth; for increased technical dexterity, applying traditional methods with

A relief on the Arch of Titus showing Jewish ritual
objects, the spoils of Jerusalem, including the great seven-
branched candlestick (*Menorah*).

new success, and making it possible to begin thinking in terms of a third dimension. It still remained for the sculptors of the Florentine Renaissance, fourteen hundred years later, to complete the conquest of the problem of perspective. But they could only do so because they had ancient models such as the Arch of Titus to study and learn from.

The spoils which the procession are carrying include the silver trumpets which the sons of Aaron had blown to summon the hosts of Israel, the golden Table of the twelve loaves of the Shewbread which were renewed in the Temple every Sabbath day, and the golden candlestick or Menorah with its seven branches – or rather six branches on a central stem. This was the most sacred object that the Jews possessed. The Lord had spoken unto Moses, saying,

'Thou shalt make a candlestick of pure gold: of beaten work shall the candlestick be made: his shaft, and his branches, his bowls, his knops, and his flowers, shall be of the same. And six branches shall come out of the sides of it; three branches of the candlestick out of the one side, and three branches of the candlestick out of the other side. . . .And thou shalt make the seven lamps thereof; and they shall light the lamps thereof, that they may give light over against it. . . . Of a talent of pure gold shall he make it, with all these vessels, and look that thou make them after their pattern, which was shewed thee in the mount.'[5]

Solomon had installed these venerated symbols in the Temple at Jerusalem. Titus seized them and took them to Rome; and now they have disappeared. Although the twelfth-century itinerary of Benjamin of Tudela asserted that Titus 'kept them in a cave near the Church of St Sebastian', they were in fact lodged in the new Temple of Peace, part of the Forum of Vespasian. But later, according to one story, while Maxentius was fleeing from Constantine (AD 312) the Menorah fell into the Tiber from the Milvian Bridge. Another report declared that Alaric the Visigoth seized the spoils when he sacked Rome a century later, and that they were buried with him in the River Bucento. But according to a more authentic version they were taken from Rome to north Africa by Gaiseric (Genseric) the Vandal when he sacked the city in 455. 'And so,' says Gibbon, 'at the end of four hundred years, the spoils of Jerusalem were transferred from Rome to Carthage by a barbarian who derived his origin from the shores of the Baltic.'

In the following century the Byzantine general, Belisarius, retrieved the precious loot and removed it to Constantinople,[6] and his emperor, Justinian, restored the principal objects to Jerusalem. But in 614 they were carried off again, this time by the Persians. They also took relics of the Holy Cross, which alone can compete with the Menorah for the mass of legends woven round its wanderings and its inviolable magical powers.

Since then the spoils have never been seen again. But there has been no lack of rumours about their fate – including a twelfth-century suggestion that they were still being kept secretly in the Lateran Palace at Rome. Lionel Davidson's novel *A Long Way to Shiloh* is constructed round the belief that the Romans never got the real Menorah at all, but were fobbed off with a fake: and that the authentic one is still hidden somewhere in Israel – fittingly enough, since it is now that country's national emblem.

Pope Paul IV introduced very stringent measures against the Jews of Rome, establishing a ghetto in the southern part of the Field of Mars and forbidding them to live in any other part of the city.[7] For centuries they gave the Arch of Titus a wide berth. But in the processions that accompanied papal installations a Jew was required to stand beside the arch in order to swear an oath of loyalty to the Pope and present him with a copy of the Pentateuch. It was not until Pius IX (1846) that the custom was discontinued. Two years later, he demolished the walls and towers of the ghetto, and the rest of it was pulled down in 1887.

## THE ARCH OF SEVERUS

The Arch of Septimius Severus (AD 193–211), at the opposite end of the Forum, is a much more elaborate affair than the Arch of Titus. Seventy-five feet high and eighty-two feet wide, it is large enough to have its interior divided into several vaulted chambers reached by an internal staircase. Moreover, the arch does not have just one single opening, but three, in accordance with a custom that came from the Greek east, where there was a tradition of multiple monumental gateways. The Arch of Severus, like the Arch of Titus, is built of Pentelic marble. Owing to the passage of centuries it stood higher than the ground level of the Republic, and the artificial, stepped base of the arch raised it to an even greater height; the base also meant that there could be no question of processions passing under it as they passed under Titus' arch. The monument of Severus had no such function. Representations

The Arch of Septimius Severus. The relief panels show Roman military triumphs including the capture of Seleucia and Ctesiphon. Through the central arch can be seen the Temple of Julius Caesar.

on coins and medallions show that it was originally crowned by statues of the emperor and his sons in a chariot of six horses, with further equestrian statues to right and left.[8] Holes at the sides of the arch suggest that shields and other metal ornaments or trophies were attached to it.

The purpose of the monument, indicated in a long inscription repeated on each of its frontages, was to celebrate the victories of Severus, his sons and his

colleagues Caracalla and Geta over the Parthians and their allies in Mesopotamia and Assyria (AD 195–9). The emperors had allegedly 'restored the Roman State and extended its empire', though in fact the campaigns were appallingly expensive in proportion to the incomplete results achieved.[9]

The occasion chosen for this celebration was the tenth anniversary of the reign (203). The name of Severus' younger son Geta, which originally appeared in the inscription near those of his father and elder brother, is no longer to be seen: for nine years after the erection of the arch, following the death of Severus at York (Eboracum), Caracalla assassinated Geta, and ordered the erasure of his name from all official inscriptions. As can be seen by looking at the fourth line, the dedication on this arch was no exception. The name of Geta is blotted out, and additional honorific titles for his murderer have replaced it.

The vaults inside the three openings are elaborately ornamented with sunk panels, and the flat spaces on either front are crammed with reliefs. As on the Arch of Titus, winged Victories are to be seen in the angles of the central curve. The angles beside the smaller lateral openings contain reclining personifications that may represent eastern rivers, the models for many a Renaissance statue. Figures of prisoners are sculptured on the bases of the columns and on the horizontal course that crowns their capitals.

But much the most important reliefs are those in the large frontal panels above the lateral arches. Unfortunately, however, they are ill-preserved; they can best be viewed from the Via del Foro Romano, on the side facing away from the Forum. These reliefs depict scenes from the eastern campaigns. Each of the four panoramas, as now reinterpreted, is concerned with a single Mesopotamian city (or in one case two cities) that provided an episode in the wars.[10] The stories have to be read in chronological order from the bottom upwards, each panel being divided into two main

*Below*, *left*: The Arch of Severus on a silver coin of his son Caracalla (*c.* AD 205).
*Below*, *right*: Relief of prisoners, their wrists chained, on the pedestals of the columns of the Arch of Severus.
*Opposite*: The coffered vault of the Arch of Titus.

zones by an irregular horizontal ground line. In the lower zones all events are contemporary, in the upper ones the sequence is from left to right.

These complex tales are very different from the self-contained pictures on the Arch of Titus. The tradition which the Severan artists follow is more reminiscent of

*Above:* Slender columns bearing reliefs decorate both sides of the Arch of Septimius Severus.
*Opposite:* The Arch of Severus marks a move away from classicism in Roman sculpture.

*Above and opposite:* The most important reliefs on the Arch of Severus are the panels above the lateral arches depicting dramatic scenes from the Eastern campaigns.

the prolonged martial narratives which wind spirally upwards round the monumental Columns of Trajan and Marcus Aurelius, both of which are still standing today – one in the Forum of Trajan close by, and the other in the Piazza Colonna, situated in the area that was formerly the Field of Mars. However, the reliefs of the Arch of Severus do not follow the *continuous* narrative method of the two Columns. This, as Richard Brilliant observes, is not a flowing epic but a series of highlighted and always significant dramatic acts.

Moreover, although the Column of Aurelius had only been completed a very few years before the Arch, it is possible to detect a stylistic development: a further move away from classicism. Already on Aurelius' column this had begun to lose its serenity. Now, on the Arch of Severus, individual human beings have become squat and insignificant: they are intended to stand for crowds rather than persons. Grouped in ceremonial tableaux which are dominated

by the emperors who declaim to their serried ranks, the figures take on the undulating rhythms of a single un-differentiated mass. The intricate division between scenes, shown at the lower levels in a bird's eye perspective, conveys the impression of a textile surface. The style was probably inspired, however, by paintings, such as those which Severus is known to have exhibited at his Triumph.[11] And those paintings in their turn may have been prompted by the popular, radical, provincial undercurrents that always flowed beneath the classical tradition, reacting against what seemed the insipid pomposity of the customary official, imperial art.

This shift of style is much more apparent on the large panels of the Arch than on its smaller reliefs. It is clearer still, and more accentuated, on a better pre-served contemporary arch at Lepcis Magna in north Africa. There is a move away from the old, classical humanism which had now degenerated into decadence – towards the two-dimensional, unplastic, frontal, rhythmically repetitive techniques of Byzantine art. A hundred years later it would be possible to design the highly un-classical statue of Constantine in the Basilica of Maxentius. But already, even now, times were changing. Severus, it is true, made great play with his inheritance of the tradition. Yet he also took large steps towards army-rule and the authoritarianism that was needed to pay for it. And the increasing anonymity of the individual human being, which is already detectable on these reliefs, forms the artistic expression of an age in which private liberties, always restricted to the higher reaches of a steep social pyramid, were beginning to vanish altogether.

A replica of this arch formed the entrance of the imperial palace at Berlin. Arcs de Triomphe and Marble Arches abound – taken from the same model and from its sequel, the Arch of Constantine which still stands beside the Colosseum. Personality cults have proved unable to resist the idea; and Sir Mortimer Wheeler has written pertinently about the Roman psychology that invented it:

If one were to seek a single emblem from the combined majesty and ostentation of successful Rome, those monstrous toys the triumphal arches were difficult to deny. It is a thought that a great people, who could drain marshes and make roads that are still our roads, build great aqueducts and shape laws that are written into our modern civilization, and after travail give a great religion and ethical code to the world, could also pause to express their self-gratification in idle contrivances of such grand but nonsensical irrelevance

# Part 3

# The Forum Since the End of Antiquity

# 9. The Destruction of the Forum

## THE MEDIEVAL FORUM

As we have seen, important reconstructions of pagan monuments continued well into the later fourth century AD; for that was the date of the Portico of the Twelve Gods in its present form (Chapter 4). The varying fates of the Altar of Victory in the Senate-house took the story of the Forum beyond 400 (Chapter 6). Evil days were now coming for Rome, which was sacked by two Germans, Alaric the Visigoth in 410 and Gaiseric or Genseric the Vandal in 455. However, the Romans claimed to have defeated subsequent Vandal marauders (*c.* 470) in a naval battle described in a dedicatory inscription which is still to be seen in the Forum today. It has been placed on a curious, ill executed, lateral extension of the New Rostra, which is believed to commemorate the same occasion. If so, this structure provides a strange final chapter to the millennial succession of victories celebrated by numberless monuments in and around the Forum.

Immediately afterwards Rome was sacked again, this time by Ricimer, half-Suebian and half-Visigoth (472). Ricimer's attack overthrew his father-in-law, the western Roman emperor Anthemius, whose gold coins have turned up, to a total of more than three hundred, in the House of the Vestals, where they had evidently been lodged to escape the looters.

After the last emperor of the west had been forced off the throne by another German, Odoacer (476), his conqueror and successor as king of Italy, Theodoric

the Ostrogoth (493–518), summoned the people to the Forum and addressed them there. He announced a new construction programme; and it was also his policy to preserve old buildings. The Senate-house was apparently one of the buildings which received a certain amount of restoration.[1] Yet it soon became wrongly known as the 'Hall of Liberty' (Atrium Libertatis), a designation that had properly belonged to the office of the Censor, housed, after various moves, in the Basilica of Trajan's Forum. The name Curia came instead, in due course, to indicate courts of law or of kings, and particularly the offices, congregations and tribunals of the Pope. Indeed, these are still grouped under the same designation today, while in canon law the college of cardinals is still the papal 'Senate'.

Other sites also changed their names. The Comitium was called the 'Three Fates', probably because there was a statue of these deities nearby;[2] and the Basilica of Maxentius was spoken of as a Temple of Rome.[3] The New Rostra ceased to be used as the official dais and the Tullianum was no longer employed as a state prison.

In the middle of the sixth century Rome suffered severely as the control of the city passed several times from Byzantines to Ostrogoths, and back again. As Byzantium's general Belisarius approached the walls, the pagan section of the Roman population made a riotous attempt to revive the ritual opening of the Temple of Janus. When the Ostrogoth Totila (541–52) plundered the city – threatening to turn it into a pasture for cows – St. Benedict declared, with only partial truth, 'Rome will not be uprooted by the nations, but will crumble and moulder away under the

Theodoric the Ostrogoth (AD 493–518) started rebuilding the ancient monuments. One of the many buildings to receive a new name was the Basilica Nova which became known as the Temple of Peace.

influence of weather, lightning, hurricanes and earthquakes.'

In 554 Rome saw its last Triumph, celebrated by the Byzantine general Narses, an elderly Armenian eunuch who defeated the Ostrogoths though he had never fought a battle before. Yet although the Byzantines conquered most of Italy, it was not long before their capital Ravenna was cut off from Rome, when the Lombards began to overrun the north of the peninsula.

A new epoch in the history of the Forum had now begun: for the first churches were being erected within the shells of the ancient monuments. Just beyond the Roman Forum, the library of the Forum of Peace or Vespasian, adjoining the 'Temple of Romulus', was transformed by Pope Felix IV (526–30) into the church of Saints Cosmas and Damian, Arabian doctors who had been victims of Diocletian's persecution. Then, after the middle of the century, the war against paganism was intensified, and places of Christian worship were built even closer to the ancient Forum Romanum itself. An Oratory to Saints Sergius and Bacchus,

Diocletianic martyrs who were revered as protectors of the Byzantine army, was built on to the Arch of Severus, and a small chapel of the Virgin was inaugurated in the library of the Temple of Caesar. These buildings have vanished, but a contemporary shrine dedicated to Saint Martina (reputedly a third-century martyr) and lodged in the archives annex of the Senate-house (Secretarium Senatus) still exists, after many reconstructions, as the lower part of the church of Saint Luke and Saint Martina.

These three buildings may all belong to the sixth century, though their exact chronology remains uncertain; and the same obscurity surrounds the date at which the guard house of Domitian's palace on the New Way was converted into the church of Santa Maria Antiqua. The interior of this shrine is still covered with paintings and repaintings of various early periods (and particularly the eighth century) which make it the finest Christian monument of the Forum. The church was said to have been dedicated on the site of a cave formerly occupied by a dragon: after slaying three hundred people with the poison of

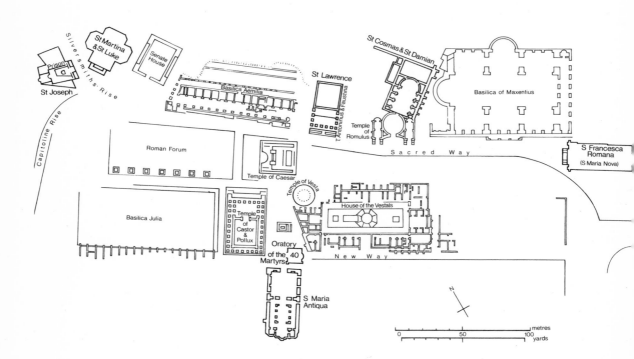

Plan of the churches on the Roman Forum, showing the sixth-century development of the site.

Wall painting from the church of Santa Maria Antiqua
beside the Forum. Forum Museum.
*Opposite:* Byzantine reliefs in the church of Santa Maria
Antiqua.

its breath, it was bound by Pope Silvester I (314–36) and shut up till the Day of Judgment.

The last traditional monument of the Forum is the Column of Phocas (602–10), a fluted Corinthian pillar forty-four feet high. It originally belonged to a building of the early imperial epoch, and its pedestal to a fourth-century structure; both column and pedestal were taken and re-erected in their present position, where the 'isolated shaft', as Longfellow called it, looks 'like a thin vapour hanging in the air, scarce visible'. Smaragdus, the Byzantine governor of Italy (exarch of Ravenna), whose record in dealing with barbarians had not been spirited, dedicated the column to his disreputable emperor Phocas. A little earlier, Pope Gregory the Great (590–604), though remaining officially loyal to the throne of Constantinople, had felt obliged to take over the practical control of Rome. Yet he wrote a complimentary letter to the new Byzantine ruler Phocas, who responded with an instruction that the patriarch of Constantinople should refrain from rivalling the Pope by using the ecumenical title. Phocas also offered the pronouncement 'that the See of the senior Apostles, Peter, is to be the head of all Churches, while the Church of Constantinople calls itself the first of all Churches' (AD 607). Another of Phocas' actions was to present the papacy with the greatest of Rome's ancient buildings, the Pantheon in the Field of Mars.

Pope Honorius I (625–38) converted the Senate-house into the church of St Adrian (finally demolished in 1937), and carried off the bronze tiles of the Basilica of Maxentius for the roof of the old St Peter's. A millennium of removing or destroying parts of the Forum had begun. Nevertheless, the construction of churches was also a potent factor in the preservation of ancient buildings. Sometimes, it is true, neither the pagan nor the Christian monument has survived,[4] but elsewhere a church has often preserved portions of the antique structure on which it had been founded.

Byzantine rule had now weakened, and an independent papal state was virtually in existence. Yet coins issued at Rome continued to bear the Byzantine imperial effigy until Pope Leo III's coronation of Charlemagne as emperor caused an open break (800). Charlemagne was crowned at Rome, but his scholarly adviser, Alcuin of York, wrote sadly of the departed splendours of the place.

Rome, once the head of the world, the world's pride,
  the city of gold,
Stands now a pitiful ruin, the wreck of its glory of old.[5]

*Above:* The column of Phocas painted by Samuel Prout (1783–1852). The column was the last monument to be erected in the Forum. City of Bristol Art Gallery.
*Opposite:* The column of Phocas today.

In 846–7 much worse was to come. In successive years the Saracens ravaged the parts of the city outside the walls, and then a serious earthquake damaged the Colosseum, half-ruined St Peter's, and caused the collapse of most of those parts of the Basilica of Maxentius which are missing today. During the

A medieval construction on the Sacred Way,
the route of
the triumphal processions of the popes.

centuries that were to follow, the building was used for hay lofts, cattle sheds, parade grounds and a riding school. Santa Maria Antiqua, beneath the huge structures of the Palatine, became unsafe after the earthquake and was abandoned in favour of Santa Maria Nova, which incorporated an Oratory of St Peter and St Paul on the Velian.[6]

The marbles and stones of the region were in tremendous demand, not only for building but for conversion into lime. In the House of the Vestals, statues of Vestal Virgins have been found all ready to be thrown on the lime-kiln; the arms, hands and feet had been hacked off and used to construct a medieval wall. The House partially fell in ruins during this period, but it continued to provide offices for papal and imperial functionaries, and its rooms have yielded a find of 830 Anglo-Saxon coins of the ninth and tenth centuries, as well as a silver pin with the name of Pope Marinus II (942–6).

In 962 Otto I inaugurated a line of Saxon monarchs who came to Rome and received the imperial crown from Popes. Otto II called himself 'Roman emperor', and Otto III (983–1002) made the city his capital. At this time the Forum was divided into four deaconries in charge of assistance to the poor. The poor needed it, for the city was now the victim of innumerable besiegers, quarrelling nobles, and murderous marauding bands. The total ruin of the Forum dates from the sack of the city by the Norman Robert Guiscard, called in to help Pope Gregory VII (1084).

After a popular rising of 1143, a building called the Novum Palatium was constructed on top of the ancient Record Office, between the Forum and Capitoline, to serve as the seat of the government of Rome, which was believed to have been conducted from here in ancient times. The old rooms were employed as a salt-store and a prison.

At this epoch the Triumphal processions of the Popes, moving from the Lateran to the Vatican, used to make their way through the Forum. Then they would pass (at a new raised ground level) beneath the Arch of Severus, which had become the principal traffic centre of the area. Other sections of the Forum were now virtually impassable. Yet a guide book of c. 1150, *Mirabilia Urbis Romae (The Wonders of the City of Rome)*, bears witness to a short breathing space, which permitted some degree of recovery from the Norman sack, and stimulated a revival of interest in the ancient monuments. *The Wonders* gives a list of these, but laces it with a strange mixture of pagan and Christian legends. Moreover, the identities of the buildings had been almost entirely forgotten; only the Temple of Saturn was still rightly described as the Treasury. The area between the Temple of Antoninus and Faustina and the Temple of Caesar (of which portions still survived) was known as the Field of Towers (Campo Torrecchiano), and one of these towers, the Torre Miranda, occupied part of the former temple, while its remaining portions housed a church dedicated to Saint Lawrence (San Lorenzo in Miranda). The northern side of the Arch of Severus was incorporated into a fortress; and at the other end of the site the same fate befell the Arch of Titus, which was built into a vast castle of the Frangipani family. Called by this name of 'bread-breakers' because they had saved the people from a great famine, they were one of the two greatest houses in Rome, possessing domains which extended as far as the Colosseum, the

The Arch of Titus painted by Ducros (1748–1810).
At that time the Arch was built into the remains of the
Frangipani Castle. National Trust, Stourhead.

Palatine and the Caelian. Their employment of the Arch of Titus to form a gate for their stronghold evidently saved it from destruction.

Near the arch was a tower known as the Turris Chartularia, because it housed the papal archives. It was demolished in 1828; but some of the Frangipani towers had disappeared as early as the thirteenth century. All such destructions accelerated the accumulation of rubbish, and so did the continuing, remorseless obliteration of ancient monuments. The debris was buried in heaps, or used as foundations for new buildings. These processes meant that the ground level continued to rise at a steady rate. Dust and rain added their normal quota of one inch a year, with larger contributions from the refuse of the squalid shacks which now extended from end to end of the Forum. Well might it be said, in those times, that Rome 'lamented the daily destruction of its ruins. Like an exhausted old man it can hardly hold itself upright on a foreign staff. Its age is honourable for nothing else but the heaps of ancient stones and the ruinous traces of the past.'

During the years when the Popes mostly resided at Avignon (1305–78), the city was at the mercy of its nobles. It was against these that Cola di Rienzi, said to be the only man who could read the old epitaphs and inscriptions, conducted a popular *coup d'état* (1347–54). After the end of his shortlived republic, the Romans were only allowed one single senator, appointed by the Pope (1358), and that is why the Novum Palatium, which had been built over the ancient Record Office, took the name of the Palace of the Senator. When the 'Babylonish captivity' at Avignon came to an end, Pope Boniface IX (1389–1404) and his successors made this building into a great castle with four corner towers, of which the two on the Forum side still remain in existence, the right-hand one being more clearly visible than its counterpart.

Captivity was followed by Schism (1378–1417), and the biographer of Eugenius IV (1431–47) remarked that 'Rome had become, by reason of the Pope's absence, like a village of herdsmen; sheep and cows wander about the city'; and just as the Capitol was known as the Mount of Goats, the Forum came to be called the *Campo Vaccino* or Field of Cows. The Temple of Castor and Pollux, which was repeatedly given different fanciful names, had already lost all the columns that are missing today, as was shown by the name of the adjoining Street of the Three Columns –

the three that are still to be seen. Illustrations of the period show them buried almost up to their capitals. Little else was visible in the Forum except the Temples of Antoninus and Faustina and of Saturn. In the fourteenth century, however, the former had lost a large amount of its walls for the reconstruction of the Lateran Palace after a fire, while part of the Temple of Saturn was torn down in 1440.

These demolitions belonged to a lengthy series. The present pitiable state of the Basilica Julia is due to authorized looting in 1413, 1426 and 1500, while equally destructive attentions were lavished on the Basilica Aemilia. It is hard to believe that there were applications to devastate these and other buildings which were not granted.

## THE FORUM IN THE RENAISSANCE

Poggio Bracciolini's work *On the Variety of Fortune* (1431) introduced a new epoch by its first-hand observation of the Forum monuments, combined with some examination of the classical writings that referred to them. Next came Flavio Biondo's *Rome Restored* (1444–6), which for all its strange identifications was the first topographical study based on a systematic attempt to relate the sites to this ancient literature. Although there was large-scale dumping of earth and rubbish round the Temple of Castor and Pollux in connection with the building of the Palazzo Venezia in the Field of Mars (1464–71), the seventies and eighties of the century witnessed attempts to detach and restore the Arches of Severus and Titus. The Jewish relief on the latter gave Mantegna (1430–1506) one of the models for his painting *The Triumph of Caesar* at Hampton Court.

Nevertheless, the later fifteenth and earlier sixteenth centuries witnessed intensified plundering. The Temples of Saturn, Vespasian and Vesta were all despoiled. Lucky finds by Pope Julius II (1503–13) stimulated the dangerous enthusiasm of excavators. The trouble was, as Thomas Ashby remarked, that 'the very men who measured and drew the remains of antiquity were most active in using them as quarries for their own buildings'. Bramante (d. 1514) plundered such travertine blocks as still survived from the Basilica Julia in order to construct the Palazzo Giraud-Torlonia across the river: and yet the same artist so admired the tunnel vaulting of the Basilica of Maxentius that he copied it in his plan for the new St Peter's.

Raphael emphasized the necessity 'of protecting the few relics left to testify to the power and greatness of that divine love of antiquity whose memory was inspiring to all who were capable of higher things'. And so, drawing up a plan of ancient Rome for Pope Leo x (1513–21), he urged that its monuments should be preserved and reconstructed, if possible in actuality or at least in drawings (1518). In the following year, when it was proposed to remove stones near the Arch of Severus, the town council sent a commission to ensure that its foundations should not be imperilled.

Under Leo x, Rome's population grew from about 70,000 to 85,000, and prosperity was also on the increase. But this progress was halted when anarchy and pillage accompanied the election of Adrian VI (1522–3), and above all when the city was sacked in 1527 by a horde of mutinous, leaderless German and Spanish soldiers who killed between 6,000 and 10,000 people and created a smoking wilderness. Even more destructive to the Forum, however, was the triumphal reception of the German emperor Charles v, to celebrate his victories in Tunis (1536). It is true that, for this occasion, Pope Paul III (1534–49) disengaged the antique porch of the Temple of Antoninus and Faustina by demolishing the medieval facade of the church of St Lawrence and three of its chapels.[7] But the Triumphal Way which he levelled between the Arches of Titus and Severus involved the obliteration of many ancient remains. The appearance of the Forum at the time, with this avenue flanked by a double row of elms, can be seen from the drawings of Marten van Heemskerck, a Fleming who spent three years in Rome (1534–6).

Pope Paul III, soon after his accession, had appointed Manetti 'to preserve all statues, inscriptions and blocks of marble, free them from brushwood and ivy, and prevent the erection of new buildings on them, or their destruction, conversion into lime, or removal from the city'. This enthusiasm produced a fresh and damaging wave of searches for works of art and inscriptions: and in spite of the threat of the death penalty for the destruction of ancient statues, the demand for building materials raged unabated. The Temple of Janus, found in 1531 and measured by the architect Labacco, had already been destroyed by Cardinal Jean Du Bellay – so that today we do not even know its site – and in 1543 excellently preserved marble portions of the Regia disappeared within thirty days of their discovery, being re-fashioned or ground up for the new St Peter's. To the same project were sacrificed the

*Top:* View of the Forum by Maarten van Heemskerck (1532–1535). Print room, State Museum, Berlin.
*Above:* Etching by Du Pérac (1575). The medieval campanile is still in place (until 1578) in the Tabularium; salt, a state monopoly, is being carried from its single open archway. Metropolitan Museum of Art, New York.

The garden of the Villa Farnese.
*Opposite:* The vestibule of the Palace of Domitian, formerly
believed to be the Temple of Augustus.

An ancient grotto which forms part of the Villa Farnese.
*Opposite:* Wall painting in the church of Santa Maria
Antiqua beside the Forum.

marble steps in front of the Temple of Antoninus and Faustina, and the marble foundations and stone walls of the Temples of Castor and Pollux and of Caesar. Perhaps it was now, also, that a decorated Doric portico at the western end of the Basilica Aemilia was demolished.

However, the surviving parts of the roof of the Basilica of Maxentius were granted to Eurialo Silvestri, who planted it with a garden which he filled with antiques (1547). The piers supporting the Basilica's dome influenced Michelangelo's designs for St Peter's. It was he, too, who established the remains of Constantine's statue, which had been taken from the Basilica Nova to the Piazza del Campidoglio at its present position in the courtyard of the Palazzo dei Conservatori. Michelangelo's successor at St Peter's, Pirro Ligorio, papal architect from 1558 to 1567, cast a strange light on the topographical ignorance of the day by arguing, with the help of over-imaginatively reconstructed inscriptions, that the real ancient site of the Forum was not where it was supposed to be at all. For he believed that it had run north and south between the Palatine and Capitoline Hills; and the correct view, put forward by Marliani, could make no headway against him.

Michelangelo's rebuilding of the Palace of the Senator, completed after his death in amended form (1582–1605), wiped out the second storey of the ancient Record Office. The austere Sixtus V (1585–9) boasted he would 'clear away the ugly antiquities'; and in 1595 Innocent IX removed a famous statue of a reclining figure from near the old prison. This was the 'Marforio', a representation of the god Oceanus, which dated from the first or second century AD and had been situated beside a great basin of grey granite (removed to the Piazza del Quirinale in 1818). This 'admirable

*Above and opposite:* Statue of the god Oceanus (Marforio) which stood by the door of the Prison, now to be seen in the courtyard of the Capitoline Museum.

The antique marble basin which stood beside the statue of Oceanus (Marforio) outside the prison.

figure Marforius', as John Evelyn called him, 'casting water into a most ample concha', had been much favoured during the sixteenth century as a 'talking' statue on which people posted anonymous subversive replies to questions inscribed the day before on another famous statue, Pasquino in the Field of Mars. Marforio is now to be seen in the courtyard of the Capitoline Museum.

The last massive column of the Basilica of Maxentius was moved to the Piazza Santa Maria Maggiore by Pope Paul V, and crowned with a statue of the Virgin (1613). Urban VIII took away one of the *cipollino* columns of the 'Temple of Romulus' and used the temple as a lower storey of the church of Saints Cosmas and Damian, raising the floor level of the church at the same time (1633). Borromini took the doors of the Senate-house, enlarged them, and moved them to the Basilica of St John Lateran (1660).

The Roman Forum as *Campo Vaccino*
or cattle market, painted by Claude Lorrain (1600–1682).
Museum of Fine Arts, Springfield, Mass.

# 10. Picturesqueness and Rediscovery

In 1627 the French landscape painter Claude Lorrain had gone to Rome. He remained there until his death in 1682, translating the atmospheric beauty of the Forum into incomparable pictures. Its desolated solitude also appealed to Alexander Pope (1688–1744).

See the wild waste of all-devouring years!
How Rome her own sad sepulchre appears,
With nodding arches, broken temples spread;
The very tombs now vanish'd like their dead.

The same ruinous picturesqueness inspired Pannini, Piranesi and many others to paintings and engravings varying from exact delineation to every sort of architectural fantasy. A particularly popular artist was the Frenchman, Hubert Robert, 'Robert of the Ruins' (1733–1808). One of his favourite subjects was the Arch of Severus, at this time buried almost up to the tops of its side arches. Its dramatic appearance also inspired the 'ruined' gateway at Prince Yusupov's Russian country-seat of Archangelskoe, the birthplace of the emperor Alexander II.

By now the ancient Forum lay under thirty, and in some places as many as forty-three, feet of rubbish. As Byron declared,

Far and wide,
Temple and tower went down, nor left a site.
Chaos of ruins!

Samuel Rogers visited Shelley and Byron at Pisa in 1820, and during the same journey he revisited Rome, which he had first seen six years earlier. In his subsequent poem *Italy*, he echoes his fellow poets' consciousness of the desolation of the scene. And yet Rogers also saw that a fresh spirit of enquiry, or at least of passionate interest, was afoot. He was conscious of this spirit in the visitors who now kept coming to the Forum:

They that would explore,
Discuss, and learnedly; or they that come
(And there are many who have crossed the earth)
That they may give the hours to meditation,
And wander, often saying to themselves,
'This was the Roman Forum!'

Such were the signs of a new epoch: for the first excavations had already begun. Indeed, they had started, on a small scale, a generation previously. The inspiration of this new kind of scientific archaeology had come from Johann Winckelmann, who first visited Rome in 1754. Ten years later, Edward Gibbon, with a lofty step, had first crossed the tree-grown Forum and began his 'cool and minute investigation' of the remains of the Roman Empire. And then the Swedish Ambassador, G. V. Fredenheim, enjoyed the distinction of launching the first dig in 1788. The area he selected was the site of the Basilica Julia.

Next, the correct topography of the Forum was largely established by Carlo Fea, starting in 1803 with the Arch of Severus. When the French occupied the city (1808–14), their Prefect, Count Tournon, conducted further excavations; Napoleon thought of restoring the Basilica of Maxentius, but decided it was too far gone. The inscription of the conspicuous Column of Phocas, Byron's 'nameless column with the buried base', was discovered in 1815, and in the following year (when Waterloo had been fought and the English were free to come back) the whole pedestal was disinterred at the expense of the intellectual Elizabeth Foster, Duchess of Devonshire, who had been painted

Painting of the Forum by Michelangelo Quercozzi
(1602–1660) showing the deeply-sunken Arch of Severus.
Minneapolis Institute of Arts.

Painting by Johann Heinrich Roos (1676),
with cattle grazing near the level of the column capitals
of the Temple of Vespasian.

by Gainsborough and now lived with Madame de Staël in a Roman palace praised as the 'salon of Europe'. Excavations of the Temples of Vespasian and of Castor and Pollux date from 1811 and 1817 respectively, and four years later Valadier, who had undertaken the former of these operations, removed the medieval accretions of the Arch of Titus and strengthened it with travertine reinforcements.

The paintings and drawings of J. M. W. Turner caught to perfection this transient moment when excavation and restoration had just started but not got very far (1819). The Forum was still essentially a rural scene; and Corot showed his feeling for the clear-cut grandeur of the Basilica of Maxentius (which had now been rightly identified) by painting it in broad masses of light and shade, more suited to its scale than the feathery softness that characterized his other Roman scenes (1825–6).[1]

*Opposite:* Pannini's painting of the Piazza Santa Maria Maggiore, the column taken from the Basilica Nova standing in front of the church in the crowded square.
*Below:* A print of the Forum by Piranesi (1720–1778), showing a scene of disorder and rusticity near the Temple of Castor and Pollux. British Museum.

A pastoral rendering of the Forum by R. L. M. de
Chancourtois (1757–1817) with ladies in
graceful poses by the Temple of Antoninus and Faustina.
Albertina, Vienna.
*Right:* Drawing by Turner (1775–1851) of the Forum in
the transitional stage when excavation had just
begun to uncover the monuments. British Museum.

204

Corot's flow of illumination transfigured the trenches and gaping holes of the excavators. But in 1834 these eyesores caused great distress to King Ludwig I of Bavaria, who loved Italy so much that he visited the country on fifty-two different occasions.

> Everywhere rents in the earth, till the eye beholds
>     nothing but chaos!
> Beautiful as it was once – not a trace of it left!
> Artists have nothing to say, archaeologists rule as they
>     please here,
> Blind to all but one side, caring for nought
>     but their own![2]

Ludwig must have been displeased if he saw the open air laundry which appears in a photograph of the Forum of about 1850.

The Portico of the Twelve Gods was largely rebuilt in 1858 with fragments found in 1834. But it was from 1870 onwards that particular energy was devoted to the rediscovery of the Forum area. At first develop-

*Below:* A painting by Corot (1796–1875) captures the bleak massiveness of the Basilica of Maxentius (or Constantine). Louvre.
*Opposite: View of Ancient Rome* by Samuel Palmer (1805–1881). City of Birmingham Art Gallery.

ments were not very rapid, for photographs of the early 1880's still show the old, greatly elevated ground level, and depict 'the meek-faced oxen of the Campagna' which, according to Augustus Hare, were 'always to be seen lying in the shade under the trees of the Forum, or drinking at its water-troughs'. But they were to be ejected before long, for Rodolfo Lanciani (1882–4) almost completed the process of laying the region bare from end to end. During a subsequent archaeological lull, Emile Zola expressed his detestation of the site as 'a long, clean, livid trench ... a city's cemetery, where old exhumed bones are whitening'.

In 1898 began the remarkable excavations of Giacomo Boni, who added centuries to the history of the Forum by discovering the Black Stone and the archaic necropolis. It was now clear that at certain points there were more than two dozen archaeological strata, one beneath the other. But Boni was also a man of artistic sensibility who wanted to make the Forum

and Palatine not only interesting but beautiful. It is to him that we owe the wistarias and ivies, roses, laurels, pink and white oleanders and white-spiked acanthuses which make this such an enchanted and fragrant place today. Boni learnt English in order to read the works of Ruskin. The two men had become friends in 1876; and Ruskin's influence intensified Boni's 'particular pleasure to heal the scars of excavation by the help of nature'.[2]

He also agreed with Ruskin's dictum 'restoration is destruction'. Since then, however, restorations have taken place. Indeed most of the buildings have now been reconstructed as far as possible; the ancient fragments have been put together, with judicious supplementation from modern materials. If that had not been done, a book such as the present one, taking its starting point from what is visible, would have had many fewer monuments to write about; and the strain imposed on the imagination by an un-reconstructed Forum would indeed have been severe.

# Appendix 1
# Building Materials of the Forum

One of the disconcerting features of the Forum, as of many Roman sites, is that the veneers of stucco and marble which covered the monuments have nearly all been stripped off long ago. Instead we see the underlying masses of stone, and even vaster masses of concrete and brick, none of which were ever supposed to be on view. Yet in another way this is helpful, for the materials that were employed changed greatly over the course of time, and one way of tracing how the Forum gradually came into existence is to keep an eye on the appearances and qualities of the various types of building material that came into use and then went out of use again, at approximately determinable dates.

The round temples of very early times, such as the Temple of Vesta in its original form, no doubt resembled contemporary human habitations, and were wattle and straw huts daubed with clay. Next, foundations of stone began to be employed. The stone used was tufa, the mixture of pebbles, lava fragments and ashes which volcanoes in the Alban hills south of the Tiber and in the Monti Cimini area to its north had spread over Latium until their activity ceased in c. 1000 BC. It was porous stone of varying hardness, but often soft enough to be worked even by early implements of bronze, a relatively ineffective metal.

The earliest colonnaded temples had columns made of wood, but they were sometimes cased in brilliant terracotta, which was also used for decorating the steep superstructures of the same buildings in styles reminiscent of the Greeks and particularly the Etruscans, who borrowed and adapted Greek ideas. Then came stone columns, coated, for protection and finish, with a stucco which was made of lime and sand and could sometimes take a high polish and moulding. Almost the only stone employed before the devasta-tion of Rome by the Gauls (c. 390 or 387 BC) was a soft, dark grey or greenish tufa called *cappellaccio*, a soft, rough, flaky and friable stone, found in the stone quarries *(lautumiae)* under the north-east side of the Capitoline Hill.[1] After the fire caused by the Gauls, *cappellaccio* continued to be used, but a greyish-yellow tufa also became available, quarried from the Grotta Oscura across the river, two and a half miles from the city on the way to Etruscan Veii, which had recently come into Roman hands. Although this stone does not weather very much better than *cappellaccio*, it was more uniform in texture and could be cut into larger blocks measuring as much as two feet long and high. Grotta Oscura tufa was exploited for two hundred years, notably for the so-called 'Servian Wall' of the fourth century BC, which surrounded the Republican city; and the same material was used for the lower cell of the prison.

This cell is also partly constructed of a harder form of tufa which is called *peperino*, because it is blackish-grey like pepper. This 'Lapis Albanus', of which the quarries were near Marino to the north of Lake Albano, possessed good fire-proof qualities. It was also harder than the Grotta Oscura tufa, and therefore more suitable for heavy lintels and vaults and column-drums. Its employment in the prison represents one of the earliest appearances of the material, but after a fire of 210 BC it began to be used extensively in the construction of temples, especially at points of particular stress and weight.

Another hard tufa, equally fireproof but flaky, came from Gabii, where the quarries are still to be seen near the fortress of Castiglione. This Lapis Gabinus or *sperone* ('spur' of a hill) was utilized a good deal during the years before and after 100 BC. Although Gabii was a dozen miles from Rome, stone could be moved to the capital by water for all but the first three miles of the journey, via the Tiber's tributary the Anio (Aniene).

A desire to economize still further in the heavy costs of transportation caused the Romans of the second century BC to experiment with a brown tufa from beside the Anio itself, just above the city. Although too rough to be suitable for ornamental cutting, this Anio tufa was as-strong as *peperino* and equally impervious to fire; it was employed to reconstruct the Great Drain and build the Record Office, and was also used for the upper storey of the prison. Ugly, but durable and inexpensive, it remained a favourite, ordinary building material for two centuries.

Another of these tufas, reddish and olive-streaked, came from Monte Verde, just across the river. Though hard and close-grained, it proved too brittle to carry heavy burdens and was abandoned before very long. But blocks of this, too, are to be seen in the upper prison; and paving slabs dating from a reconstruction by the dictator Sulla (d. 78 BC) are visible in the Forum itself, where they were placed on top of previous pavement levels. These had consisted of other tufas or of beaten gravel. The earliest street pavement to have survived belongs to the Capitoline Rise (174 BC). Its blocks of basaltic lava *(silex)*, quarried the other side of Falerii, are full of crystals to help give a hold on the steep roadway.

Another innovation of the same period was the use of travertine. A large supply of this strong limestone was discovered during the second century BC near Aquae Albulae (Bagni), fourteen miles from Rome on the road to Tibur, the modern Tivoli. Owing to the level nature of the ground and its dense vegetation, the quarries had escaped observation hitherto. Still in abundant use today, this stone is rather soft when first exposed, which makes it easy to saw and work; soon afterwards it hardens. Travertine was used for the external lintel and capitals of the Record Office, and by the time of Caesar its notable structural advantages were being fully exploited. It was also employed for street-curbs, and travertine flags replaced tufa as the paving of the Forum. Moreover this same stone, which weathers from a greyish-white or greyish-yellow to a rose-brown or honey tint, proved scarcely inferior to marble as a facing.

But the greatest and most influential of all the discoveries of this productive second century BC was concrete. That is what enabled the Romans, or the foreign architects they employed, to advance far beyond what Greece had ever taught them. The uses of concrete are readily visible in the Forum area. First of all it appears in the bases of the Temples of Concord and of Castor and Pollux (121, 117 BC) – massive foundations so skilfully made that they suggest a considerable period of earlier experimentation, which we cannot now trace. Next comes the employment of the same material as a bedding for street pavements and brick walls and as a backing of vaults (in the upper chamber of the prison). More ambitious was the massive concrete vaulting of the Record Office; and far more imposing still are the immense arches of the Basilica Nova of Maxentius.

Adhesives of sand, mixed with lime and water, were already known to Cretans of the second millennium before our era. By 250 BC, if not before, such techniques had become familiar to the Greek cities of southern Italy. Early in the following century, Romans discovered that an excellent material for this purpose was provided by a natural pulverized volcanic blend of cinders and clay. It is known as *pozzolana* because of its particular abundance at Puteoli (Pozzuoli near Naples), but quantities are also found within a short distance of the eastern and southern gates of Rome itself. When lime was added to *pozzolana* in a kiln, the molten mortared mass became an exceptionally consistent and coherent concrete, which was poured over a rubble 'aggregate' made from chips of stone and brick and sometimes (for the sake of lightness) pumice. The result was a compact monolithic mass – at which, as the elder Pliny said, one cannot marvel enough.[2] Extraordinarily resistant to strains and stresses, it was nearly indestructible, and exerted no lateral thrust. Gradually, successive generations awoke to its breathtaking potentialities for the construction of soaring vaults and arches and apses.

During the influx of wealth derived from Rome's conquests during the second century BC, various marbles came into use in the city. Quintus Metellus Macedonicus, returning from service in Greece, employed a Greek architect (and perhaps Greek materials) to build two marble-faced temples in the Field of Mars, just outside the walls (148 BC). Then Sulla and Caesar, when they reconstructed the Forum, made abundant use of the same material. A few wealthy nobles of the Republic also began to import exotic marbles for the porticoes of their own houses. In the Forum area today, though most of the veneers have long since been ransacked, the Pentelic marble casing of the monumental arches remains. Variegated marble pavements can also still be seen, and marble columns, the green-banded *cipollino* ('onion') from Carystus in Euboea being particularly well represented; and the Temple of Saturn displays two kinds of granite. In the time of Augustus, the whole of the Forum was brilliant with many-coloured marbles, including the glaring white products of the Carrara quarries which he was the first to exploit on a large scale.

Augustus claimed to have found Rome brick and left it marble – a boast almost justified as regards its public buildings, though by no means true of private houses, which remained slummy until Nero attempted to improve them. But even the public buildings continued to be made of brickwork underneath, as we can see today from the immense heaps and lumps of the material which still exist, naked and stripped of their rich outer covering. The Republic had used unbaked bricks faced with stucco, especially for private houses, but naturally very few remnants of this short-lived material have survived. By the beginning of the empire, however, this crude brick had been replaced by more durable kiln-baked varieties, first irregular, next square or diamond-shaped ('reticulate'), then for centuries flat and rectangular. The bricks covered the concrete, and were themselves covered by the marble. The heat-resisting qualities of Roman brick were demonstrated in the fires that devastated Rome under Nero (64) and again under Commodus (191) and Carinus (283), giving successors of the two last named, Severus and Diocletian, opportunities to emulate Nero and embark on further vast schemes of reconstruction of their own.

From the second century AD, bricks were being designed to serve as outer facings in their own right – they were being made, that is to say, to be seen, in final rejection of the Greek heritage of stone exteriors.

*Below:* Reconstruction of the Arch of Augustus drawn to illustrate the remaining fragments.
*Opposite left:* The Arch of Augustus as rebuilt in 19 BC depicted on a silver *denarius*.
*Opposite right:* The Arch of Augustus (29 BC) on a silver coin issued by Octavian (Augustus) in the East.

# Appendix 2
# Vanished Monuments

In the foregoing chapters, to avoid confusion, little has been said about the very numerous buildings in the Forum which have either disappeared altogether or have only survived in fragments or traces. But it may be useful to list some of the most important of these monuments here.

ARCH OF AUGUSTUS. This single-columned arch was built in 29 BC, after the battle of Actium, just beyond the SE end of the Forum, linking the Temple of Caesar with the Temple of Castor and Pollux. In 19 BC, after the recovery of captured standards from Parthia, it was transformed into a three-arched monument, which at that time was still a rare architectural feature. In this form it is shown on a coin issued in 16 BC.[1] Only foundations and fragments exist today.

ARCH OF FABIUS. This monument stood on the Sacred Way, NE of the Temple of Caesar, and marked the boundary of the actual open space of the Forum. It was erected by Quintus Fabius Maximus Allobrogicus from the spoils of his Gallic victories (121 BC). This arch had no columns, i.e. it was a simple *fornix* or span and not an *arcus* in the correct sense of the term. Remnants of the travertine base survive.

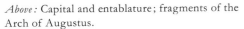

*Above:* Capital and entablature; fragments of the Arch of Augustus.

*Above right:* Detail of sculpted relief on the Arch of Constantine showing the Arch of Tiberius in the background.

*Opposite:* The Schola Xanthi foundations; this Office of the Scribes and Heralds of the Aediles was rebuilt by both Tiberius and Caracalla.

ARCH OF JANUS. See Temple of Janus.

ARCH OF TIBERIUS. Consisting of a single arch, led up to by a flight of steps, the Arch of Tiberius stood below the Temple of Saturn at the SW corner of the Forum, beside the beginning of the Street of the Yoke-Makers. It was built by Tiberius in AD 16, to celebrate the recapture by Germanicus of the legionary eagles lost with Varus to the Germans seven years earlier. This monument appears on a relief on the Arch of Constantine. The concrete foundation survives.

BASILICA OPIMIA. It was built at the N extremity of the area beneath the Capitoline Hill, between the Temple of Concord and the prison, by Lucius Opimius, a conservative leader, after the murder of his political enemy Gaius Gracchus (121 BC). Opimius also rebuilt the Temple of Concord (q.v.); its further reconstruction by Tiberius was what probably caused the demolition of this Basilica.

BASILICA PORCIA. This, the earliest Basilica in Rome, was erected in the face of opposition by Cato the Elder (184 BC), in the area of the stone quarries (*lautumiae*), just W of the Senate-house. It was burnt down, together with the Senate-house, in the riots accompanying the funeral of Clodius in 52 BC.

BASILICA SEMPRONIA. Built in 170 BC by Tiberius Gracchus, father of the famous Gracchi, on property of Scipio Africanus the Elder. Replaced by Caesar's Basilica Julia, but various remnants survive; others go back to even earlier buildings on the same site.

GOLDEN HOUSE OF NERO (AD 54–68). Although the main building was on the Esquiline Hill, ruins along the Velian slope s and e of the Forum belong to the mile-long colonnade which formed its vestibule (being built over Nero's earlier Domus Transitoria spanning Esquiline and Palatine). The portico was divided into three sections by the New Way and the Sacred Way – which was endowed by Nero with monumental arcades leading up to the vestibule of the palace. However, the fragmentary, surviving travertine piers and concrete cores of the vestibule are hard for the visitor to find among the encumbering debris and attractive vegetation (which one would not want to lose), and guide-books are of no assistance.

The Colossus of Nero, a statue executed by Zenodorus who was the leading sculptor of the day, stood in a colonnaded courtyard at the mid-part of the vestibule, rising to a height of 110 or 120 feet. Its crown of rays compared or identified Nero with the Sun, a deity with whom he was frequently equated in contemporary adulation[2]. The cult of the Sun received special honours after his detection of Piso's conspiracy (AD 65). Vespasian replaced the head of the Colossus by a conventional head of the Sun which no longer resembled Nero, and Hadrian had the statue moved into the valley (by 24 elephants, under the direction of a special architect) in order not to obstruct his Temple of Venus and Rome on the Velian. The architect of

this temple, Apollodorus, was ordered to erect a twin statue of the Moon. The Sun-statue that had once represented Nero came to be regarded with superstitious awe as a guarantee of Rome's eternity, and a custom grew up of placing flowers round it once a year. In the Middle Ages the neighbouring Flavian Amphitheatre was named after it – and called the Colosseum.

OFFICE OF THE SCRIBES AND HERALDS OF THE AEDILES. Low arches SW of the New Rostra, projecting from the lower slopes of the Capitoline Hill, have been identified by an inscription found in the sixteenth century as parts of this building. The structure was rebuilt by Tiberius and again by Caracalla, and is known as the Schola Xanthi from the name of one of the dedicators of Tiberius' reconstruction.

SHRINE OF FAUSTINA THE YOUNGER (Aedicula Faustinae). Beneath the Capitoline Hill between the Temples of Concord (see below) and Vespasian. Statue-base survives. The younger Faustina, wife of Marcus Aurelius, died and was deified in AD 175.

SHRINE OF VULCAN (Vulcanal). This place, sacred to Vulcan, is a small area on the lower slopes of the Capitoline Hill behind the New Rostra. A base which may have belonged to the original open-air altar is cut out of the natural tufa, and the precinct was bounded by tufa blocks. Originally larger in size than its present size of thirteen by nine feet, the area contained a lotus tree and a cypress believed to be older than the city itself. Roots of the lotus were said to reach as far as the other end of the Senate-house. The shrine of Vulcan also possessed a statue of Romulus (inscribed 'in Greek letters'), in addition to a sculptured representation of a four-horse chariot which was said to have been dedicated by that monarch.

For this, according to tradition, was the place where Romulus and Tatius concluded the peace between the Latins and Sabines, bringing about the merger between the hill-villages which resulted in the foundation of the Roman state.[3] Whatever the truth of these early happenings – which would be attributable to about the eighth century BC – the Vulcanal became the Assembly place of the monarchy in the days before the Comitia and Old Rostra existed. Before that, it may already have been a place of worship, for this was a type of open-air shrine which originated in the days before Rome had become a town at all. The Vulcanal

Archaic statuettes in the Forum Museum; the first figure on the left is an *augur* (possibly Attus Navius) with his curved staff (*lituus*).

owes its position here in the Forum, outside the boundaries of the original villages, to the fact that Vulcan, being a god of fire, was too destructive to be anywhere near human habitations. Identified with the Greek fire-god Hephaestus, he was mainly worshipped in order to avert fires, which were particularly feared at the time of his annual festival in August, when the storehouses were full of new grain. Augustus embellished the site with an altar which is now in the Naples Museum (AD 9), and Domitian presented a new marble-faced altar, sacrificing a red calf and a boar.

STATUE OF ATTUS NAVIUS. This stood on the steps to the left of the Senate-house. He was a legendary priest (*augur*) believed to have cut a whetstone in two in order to dispose of King Tarquinius Priscus' doubts about the validity of the ritual of the auspices.[4] Nearby grew the Fig-tree of Navius, reputed to have been the tree which had sheltered the infants Romulus and Remus and was then miraculously brought here from the Lupercal (Palatine) by the augur. It was regarded as a symbol of Roman power. In AD 59 alarm was caused because the tree began to wither; but it revived. The site, which was surrounded by a bronze grating, may have marked a spot struck by lightning.

STATUE OF CONSTANTINE THE GREAT on horseback. A quadrilateral brick base (originally faced with marble) on the SE side of the Forum was probably the pedestal of this vast image.

STATUE OF DOMITIAN on horseback. Erected to commemorate his victories on the northern frontiers (c. AD 91–2), this stood on an enormous base, near the statue just mentioned. The concrete foundation is still visible, also three travertine blocks which supported the horse's feet. The subject of a sycophantic poem by Statius,[5] the statue stood on top of a prehistoric holy place: antique objects were found on the site by the constructors of Domitian's statue, and they were deliberately left enclosed in the statue's base. After his murder, it suffered the fate of his numerous other statues, and was overthrown.

STATUE OF TREMULUS. This statue of Quintus Marcius Tremulus, wearing a toga without a tunic and riding on a horse, stood in front of the Temple of Castor and Pollux and commemorated his victory over the Italian tribe of the Hernici (300 BC). It may have been the first equestrian statue in Rome.

STATUE OF VERTUMNUS, god of orchards and fruit. This seems to have stood behind the SE corner of the Basilica Julia, on Tuscan Street. The base of the statue was found in 1549. Vertumnus' annual festival was celebrated on 13 August, when the fruit was ripe.

> Of Tuscan origin am I,
> Yet grieve not that from Tuscany
> Mid war's alarms I came to Rome
> Deserting my Volsinian home.
> Its busy crowds I love to see:
> No ivoried fane has charms for me …
> But, Father of the Gods, I pray
> That I in Rome may stand for aye,
> And evermore the togas greet
> That pass in thousands at my feet.[6]

STATUES of other gods and men abounded. For example, a row of seven brick bases dating from the fourth century AD is still visible in front of the Basilica Julia. On these stood columns bearing the effigies of honoured citizens, like the nearby Column of Phocas which was surmounted by an image of that emperor. Parts of two of these columns have now been re-erected. Beside the Sacred Way, in 1882, were found pedestals dedicated to four emperors and a city-prefect of AD 339. The Capitoline Rise, too, was thickly lined with statues.

*Left:* The Temple of Augustus with statues of himself and his wife Livia; Antoninus Pius announces its restoration (AD 157–8).
*Centre:* Bronze medallion of Antoninus Pius supposedly showing the Temple of Bacchus conjecturally identified near the Forum.
*Right:* The Temple of Concord on a brass coin of Tiberius (AD 14–37).

TEMPLE OF AUGUSTUS. This temple in honour of the deified Augustus was completed by Tiberius or Caligula, and dedicated by the latter. Later it was destroyed by fire and restored by Antoninus Pius, as his coins record. It contained statues of Augustus and his wife Livia, and then of later deified emperors as well. The temple stood somewhere to the south of the Basilica Julia, since the bridge by which Caligula linked his Palatine palace with the Capitol passed over its roof.[7] However, in spite of suggested attributions, its exact site remains unknown.

TEMPLE OF BACCHUS. Opposite the Basilica of Maxentius is a fragment of a lintel of the second or third century AD decorated with the figure of a Maenad. This may come from a Temple of Bacchus (identified with Dionysus and Liber) which was known to have been situated on the Sacred Way, and was restored, as an inscription shows, by Antoninus Pius.

Alternative interpretations ascribe these remains to a Temple of Cybele (the Asian earth-mother) or the Penates.

TEMPLE OF CONCORD. Its massive concrete base can be seen from the Via del Foro Romano, NE of the Temple of Vespasian, beside the substructure of the Record Office. Concordia, an adaptation of the Greek Homonoia, was the power which held all Romans together in times of stress – the earliest known Roman example of the personifications that had become a commonplace of Greek thought.

The temple was built by Camillus in 367 BC to commemorate the historic reconciliation between patricians and plebeians. The terracotta figure of Victory at the apex was struck by lightning in 211 BC, but it was caught in its fall by another statue of Victory on the pediment. Lucius Opimius restored the building in 121, to urge harmony after the murder of

*Opposite:* Cornice of the Temple of Concord: now in the gallery of the Record Office (Tabularium).
*Below:* Imaginative reconstruction of the Temple of Janus, which stood near the portico of the Basilica Aemilia.

*Bottom:* Coin of Nero showing the Temple of Janus. This issue celebrated one of the rare times of peace during which the doors of the Temple of Janus were traditionally closed.

Gaius Gracchus. The base, dating from this restoration, displays the earliest known use of concrete at Rome.

During the late Republic the Senate often met in this temple, and it was the scene of Cicero's stirring Fourth Catilinarian Oration[9] – the building provided a convenient symbol of national unity, and was located suitably close to the Tullianum gaol, to which the conspirators were conducted immediately afterwards to be put to death.

Another reconstruction of the temple took place during the reign of Augustus. It was the work of his heir-apparent Tiberius, who re-dedicated the shrine in his own name and the name of his late brother, Drusus the elder, in order to symbolize the concord that prevailed between the members of the imperial house (AD 7–10). The ground plan of this restoration still remains. Tiberius' building, like the Temple of Caesar, is seen to have been wider than it was deep, owing to its cramped position at the foot of the Capitoline Hill. His reconstruction is displayed on his coins of AD 34–6, celebrating the 400th anniversary of the first foundation,[10] and it likewise appears on a second century relief in the Vatican. A considerable part of the rich entablature of the building can be seen in the gallery of the Record Office, and there are also remains in the Capitoline Museum. Tiberius and Livia endowed the temple with a valuable collection of Greek sculpture.

TEMPLE OF JANUS (Quirinus or Geminus). Adjoining the SW corner of the Basilica Aemilia, where the Argiletum leaves the Forum. Its exact site is uncertain, but has been conjecturally determined by the position of two *peperino* blocks. The Byzantine historian Procopius described the temple as a tiny rectangular sanctuary, with doors at either end, and side walls faced with bronze.[11]

In the interior of the Temple stood a bronze statue of Janus Bifrons, i.e. with two faces, looking both ways. The temple contained twelve small altars dedicated to the twelve months, starting with Janus' own month January, which replaced March in 153 BC as the first month of the year. Mentioned at the start of certain prayers, as Vesta was mentioned at their end, Janus was the power of beginnings – the 'god of gods' of an antique hymn. His name was connected with *ianua*, the door of a house or gate of a town.

There was a lucky and an unlucky way of setting out. In starting forth to war the magic of Janus was needed; and the doors of his shrine were only closed in time of peace – when war was regarded as imprisoned inside them. Coins of Nero, which provide a sketch of the temple, specifically celebrate one of the rare occasions on which such a closure was possible.[12]

Possibly the temple originated as a double gate to one of the primitive villages that preceded Rome, and subsequently became a symbolic entrance to the Forum. Although Livy assigns the building to the antique age of Numa Pompilius (traditionally eighth century BC),[13] its bronze coating suggests a date round about 500. For this feature is reminiscent of the Temple of Athena Chalkioikos of Sparta, which could well have become known to the Romans at that time through their relations with Sparta's 'colony' in south Italy, Taras (Tarentum). In 260 BC another temple was vowed to Janus in the Field of Mars, and altars to Janus, Peace and Well-Being (Salus) were erected in 11 BC in the quarter-millenary year after that date.[14]

A favourite resort of the money-changers and bankers (like the Well-head of Libo, q.v.), was known as 'Middle Janus' or 'Janus in the middle'.[15] Since Livy speaks of an Italian town erecting 'three Jani',[16] it has been supposed that there were also three at Rome, and that Horace's allusion to 'Janus from the highest to the lowest'[17] refers to them. This is probably correct, but it does not seem justifiable to conclude that all the three monuments were concentrated in the Roman Forum. Instead they seem to have been disposed along the transverse axis of the Great Drain, at points where there had been ancient bridge heads at a time when the Drain was still a stream. One of these Januses seems to have lain north of the Forum and one south of it (near the Tiber), and 'Middle Janus' is probably to be identified with the Temple of Janus referred to in the previous paragraphs. If this interpretation is right, the temple marked the original bridge at the point where the brook (the later drain) flowed across the deep valley that later became the Roman Forum.

TRIBUNAL OF AURELIUS. One of the numerous tribunals for legal cases, apparently to the SE of the Forum: possibly on the site later occupied by the platform in front of the Temple of Caesar. This tribunal was erected in the first half of the last century BC, perhaps by Marcus Aurelius Cotta (consul 74 BC). Cicero, who also calls it the Aurelian Steps (*gradus*), implies that this was a centre where Jews congregated. He also refers to it as a point where Clodius levied gangs of slaves and other toughs before his own murder in 52 BC.[18]

TRIBUNAL OF THE CITY PRAETOR (*praetor urbanus*). Site disputed. Ancient commentators believed it was beside the Well-head of Libo (q.v.), but this assumption may be unjustified. The annual post of city praetor, according to tradition, was created in 366 BC (the first praetorship to be brought into existence) in order to supervise the administration of justice. Later this official concentrated on lawsuits between Roman citizens. Like other senior officials, he had the right to proclaim by edicts the legal principles that he intended to follow during his year of office. During the last century of the Republic, the edict of the city praetor (retained from year to year, with amendments) became the main instrument for the development of the law. A revised codification of these edicts was issued by Salvius Julianus in *c.* 130 AD.

Inscription of Lucius Naevius Surdinus, praetor dealing
with foreign cases at the beginning of the Empire.

The Well-Head of Libo (Puteal Libonis, Scribonianum)
on a *denarius* of Lucius Scribonius Libo, *c.* 55 BC.

By that time the tribunals had been largely super-
seded by the Basilicas and Imperial Fora, though some
of the ancient platforms still existed at the beginning
of the empire. But many of them had never been more
than wooden structures; and whenever there was
trouble – for instance at the cremations of Clodius and
Caesar – they tended to be broken up to provide fuel
for the flames.

TRIBUNAL OF THE PRAETOR DEALING WITH
FOREIGNERS. In the pavement of the Forum, near
the Column of Phocas, there is an inscription, originally in metal letters (now restored), naming Lucius
Naevius Surdinus, praetor 'between citizens and
foreigners', i.e. the *praetor peregrinus* who dealt with
lawsuits in which at least one of the parties was a
foreigner. Surdinus lived at the beginning of the
empire, but long before that (perhaps from the
creation of the post in 242 BC) there had been a
peregrine praetor's tribunal here, and the inscription
seems to commemorate its restoration by Tiberius –
though perhaps largely as an antiquarian site, since so
much of the court work was now done elsewhere. The
tribunal probably comprised a low platform which
could be covered by a canopy. This was the place
where many of the principles that helped to create
international law were formulated.

VULCANAL. See Shrine of Vulcan.

WELL-HEAD OF LIBO. (Puteal Libonis or Scribonianum.) This so-called well-head, of which tufa and
travertine remains have now been found under the
Arch of Augustus between the Temples of Caesar and
Castor, marked a fenced-off sacred place. It may have
been the site of an ancient well, but it might instead
be a point where lightning had struck: the word
*puteal* first meant a stone-curb round a well, but then
came to signify a similar erection round sacred spots
of other kinds. This well-head, whether rightly or
wrongly so called, was named after a certain Lucius
Scribonius Libo, who, at an unknown date, reconstructed this little monument; its appearance is reproduced on the late Republican coinage of a member of
his family.[19] The place was a Roman Exchange, where
the business men of Rome were accustomed to con-
gregate.[20] Another point where they assembled was
the Temple of Janus (q.v.), and they had offices at a
location between these two meeting-places, in the
New Shops in front of the Basilica Aemilia.

# Notes

PART I

## THE CENTRE OF THE WORLD

CHAPTER I
THE LIFE OF THE FORUM

1. Suetonius, *Divus Julius*, 372
2. Dio Cassius, LX, 23, 1; cf. XLIII, 21, 1f. for Caesar
3. Livy, XXIII, 30
4. Or the purpose of the windlasses may have been to move heavy weights along the Forum
5. *Res Gestae Divi Augusti*, 22
6. Pliny the elder, *Historia Naturalis*, XIX, 23
7. For this and other streets leading into the Forum, see below, Chapter 2
8. Plautus, *Curculio*, 467–82. Line 4: the eighteenth century translator (B. Thornton, 1772), renders 'Comitium' as law-courts. Line 5: Cloacina's shrine was on the NE edge of the Forum. Line 7: 'Exchange' is 'basilica': but there was none before the Basilica Porcia, erected in the year of Plautus' death, so that this line has been regarded as a later addition. Line 9: the fish-market (like the sweet-shops) was absorbed by a large market built in 179 BC, NE of the Forum and the new Basilica Aemilia)
9. Paulus Diaconus, *Epitome of Festus*, p. 134 Müller
10. There was also another luxury market N of the Sacred Way, near the Subura, called the Forum of Desire

(*Cuppedinis*), Varro, *De Lingua Latina*, V, 186
11. Plutarch, *Galba*, XXVII
12. Ammianus Marcellinus, XVI, 13, 1

CHAPTER 2
THE BEGINNINGS OF THE FORUM

1. Tacitus, *Annals*, XII, 24 gives too early a date for the settlement; so does the myth that it was founded by Saturn
2. The modern Lazio extends on both its banks
3. Varro, *De Lingua Latina*, V, 148–50
4. Ovid, *Fasti*, VI, 395–416
5. Horace, *Odes*, I, 2, 13–16
6. One little piece of gold has turned up under the equestrian statue of Domitian
7. Dionysius of Halicarnassus, II, 50, 2, places this stage too early, under Romulus
8. Livy, I, 38, 6 (Tarquinius Priscus)
9. Suetonius, *De Grammaticis*, 2
10. For this and other building materials, see Appendix 1
11. By the Clivus Palatinus (Palatine Rise): see also next note
12. 'Rise' may seem a slightly unnatural term, but there are parallels for it and I can find no better equivalent for 'Clivus'
13. Between the Temple of Vesta and Spring of Juturna
14. Virgil, *Aeneid*, VIII, 346
15. Varro, Dionysius of Halicarnassus
16. Aeneas was believed to have founded it in honour of his wife Lavinia, daughter of Latinus. He was

then, according to the legend, succeeded by his son Ascanius, who founded Alba Longa where, after twelve more reigns, a descendant gave birth to Romulus and Remus
17. *Corpus Inscriptionum Latinarum*, VI, 36840

PART 2

## THE BUILDINGS OF THE FORUM

CHAPTER 3
THE MOST SACRED PRECINCT

1. Like three Roman shrines of another early deity, Hercules
2. Ovid, *Fasti*, VI, 261f. (translated by John Gower, 1640)
3. 513, 241, 210 BC; 64, 191 AD
4. Servius on Virgil, *Aeneid*, VIII, 190
5. Cicero, *De Natura Deorum*, II, XXVII, 67
6. Tacitus, *Annals*, XV, 36 (tr. M. Grant). According to another account Nero first caught the fringe of his robe, and regarded this as a bad omen
7. Ovid, *Fasti*, VI, 295f.
8. Cassius Hemina, fragment 5 Peter, cf. Servius on Virgil, *Aeneid*, III, 12
9. In April the blood was distributed as one of the materials for purifying cattle-stalls
10. Not the version followed by Virgil, *Aeneid*, II, 162–79
11. *Scriptores Historiae Augustae*, *Antoninus Elagabalus*, VI, 8f.

12. Plutarch, *Camillus*, 20
13. Livy IV, 44, 11f. (tr. J.P.V.D. Balsdon)
14. The Porta Capena: Spring of the Camenae and Egeria
15. Macrobius, *Saturnalia*, III, 13, 11
16. Dio Cassius, LI, x, 3 (Caligula); cf. Tacitus, *Annals*, IV, 16 (Tiberius)
17. Herodian V, 6, 2, Dio Cassius, LXXX, 9, 3
18. Beside the Porta Collina
19. Solinus, *Collectanea*, I, 21
20. Dionysius of Halicarnassus, II, 70
21. Macrobius, *Saturnalia*, I, 10

CHAPTER 4
SHRINES FOR THE GODS

1. Porphyry, *De Abstinentia*, II, 54
2. Attributed to Pythagoras of Rhegium
3. For this and other building materials see Appendix 1
4. Cicero, *In Verrem*, II, i, 145: or *tectorium* might refer to paint or whitewash
5. *British Museum Catalogue, Coins of the Roman Empire*, Vol. V, p. 196, no. 216 (Geta)
6. Ammianus Marcellinus, XIX, 11, 4
7. Justin XX, 3, 8, cf. Suidas
8. Varro, *De Re Rustica*, I, 2, 9
9. Lex Bantia: probably *c.* 104–100 BC
10. Cicero, *In Verrem*, II, i, 129
11. Plutarch, *Cato Minor*, 26ff.
12. Cicero, *De Haruspicum Responsis*, XXIII, 49, cf. *Pro Milone*, VII, 18
13. In the Temple of Juno Moneta
14. Suetonius, *Gaius*, 21, 2
15. Pliny, *Historia Naturalis*, XXXVI, 11
16. For bricks of this shape (reticulate), see Appendix 1
17. Marcus Barbatius Pollio, curule aedile
18. Virgil, *Aeneid*, XII, p. 123
19. Arnobius, III, p. 123
20. There is an alternative view that the statues stood on top of the colonnade
21. Livy, XXII, 10
22. Ammianus Marcellinus, XXX, 9, 5

CHAPTER 5
SHRINES FOR THE CAESARS

1. Right: Arch of Augustus (Appendix 2). Left: an arch over the Sacred Way linking the temple with the chapel of Augustus' grandsons Gaius and Lucius at the end of the arcade of the Basilica Aemilia
2. Suetonius, *Divus Julius*, 84, 3; Appian, *Civil Wars*, II, 148
3. Plutarch, *Brutus*, 20, 4f. (tr. B. Perrin)
4. Suetonius, *Divus Julius*, 88
5. Augustus, *Res Gestae*, 21
6. Ovid, *Metamorphoses*, XV, 840 (tr. H. Gregory)
7. Diodorus Siculus, VI, 1f., V, 41f.
8. Tacitus, *Annals*, I, 8
9. Frontinus, *De Aquis Urbis Romae*, 129 (9 BC). This was in replacement of the Temple of Castor and Pollux
10. Trajanus Decius or Trebonianus Gallus
11. For this and other building materials see Appendix 1
12. Cf. Latin coins of Bithynian Apamea: M. Grant, *Roman History from Coins*, pl. 28, no. 3
13. Claudian, *On the Third Consulship of Honorius*, 105ff., cf. 158ff., still refers to the immortality of good emperors
14. Other suggestions are: Temple of the Sacred City, Temple of the Di Penates, vestibule of the Forum of Peace

CHAPTER 6
THE MEETING PLACES OF PEOPLE AND SENATE

1. Livy, VIII, 14
2. Caesar planned and Agrippa (under Augustus) completed a new voting place for them there, the Saepta Julia
3. Plutarch, *Brutus*, 20, 3f. (tr. B. Perrin)
4. Suetonius, *Augustus*, 65
5. Dio Cassius, LVI, 34
6. Servius on Virgil, *Aeneid*, III, 20; cf. IV, 58
7. Pliny the elder, *Historia Naturalis*, VII, 12
8. *Codex Theodosianus*, IX, 7, 6

9. Cicero, *In Catilinam*, I, 2
10. Tacitus, *Annals*, I, 7
11. Ammianus Marcellinus, XVI, 10, 5
12. Cf. Anonymus, *Carmen adversus Flavianum*; and Ostia inscription of Numerius Projectus (*Harvard Theological Review*, XXXVIII, 1945, p. 201)
13. Claudian, *On the Sixth Consulship of Honorius*, 597, and *On the Second Consulship of Stilicho*, 204

CHAPTER 7
VAULTS AND ARCADES

1. It is also possible, however, that the beams were installed temporarily as a scaffold for the vaulting
2. For these materials, see Appendix 2
3. Gellius, *Noctes Atticae*, III, 3, 15
4. Sallust, *Bellum Catilinae*, LV, 4
5. These are sometimes attributed to the Tuscan Order, which was a version of Doric with column-bases, simple entablatures, and unfluted columns: but here there are traces of fluting.
6. On the Capitol the rectangle was broken to leave room for the antique Temple of Vejovis. During the construction of an underground passage linking the palaces of the Piazza del Campidoglio other large portions of the exterior of the Record Office have come to light. Much is visible on the NE side (Via di S. Pietro in Carcere)
7. E.g. below the Arch of Tiberius, in front of the Temple of Saturn
8. For this and other building materials see Appendix 1
9. Virgil, *Georgics*, II, 501
10. Tacitus, *Histories*, III, 71
11. Livy, XXXIX, 44
12. Varro, *De Lingua Latina*, VI, 4
13. *British Museum Catalogue, Coins of the Roman Republic*, I, no. 3650
14. Pliny the elder, *Historia Naturalis*, XXXVI, 121ff.
15. Chronographer of the Year 354 (*Monumenta Germaniae Historica*, IX, 1892, p. 145)
16. Quintilian, X, i, 119
17. Pliny the younger, *Epistles*, II, 11, 14; cf. VI, 33 for acoustics
18. Behind these buildings, on Tuscan

Street, are considerable remains of the warehouses (Horrea) of Agrippa and Germanicus, originally surrounding three courtyards, one of which contains a shrine

19. Fifty-four spiral steps led up to the roof

20. The apse of the shrine of Rome, the better preserved of the two, can be seen from the Forum Museum

21. Eusebius, *Ecclesiae Historia*, IX, 9, 7

## CHAPTER 8
### THE MONUMENTAL ARCHES

1. Livy, XXXIII, 27

2. Though *arcus* is also used loosely in this sense, e.g. Seneca, *De Constantia Sapientis*, I

3. Pliny the elder, *Historia Naturalis*, XXXIV, 27

4. Possibly the Arch was not finished until the time of Trajan (AD 98–117)

5. *Exodus*, XXV, 31f., 37, 39f. The 'knops' of this Authorized Version were carvings of flower-buds; a talent was about 108 lb. of gold. For the trumpets see *Numbers*, X, 1–10. The Table of the Shewbread on the Arch was believed in the Middle Ages to be the Ark. Josephus, *Antiquitates Judaicae*, III, 6, 7 explains that the Menorah was of cast gold, and hollow

6. Procopius, *Bellum Vandalicum*, IV, 9, 5ff.

7. They had been settled in a larger area in the same district since the previous century. In ancient times their quarter had been across the river

8. *British Museum Catalogue, Coins of the Roman Empire*, IV, p. 216, no. 320

9. Dio Cassius, LXXV, 3, 3

10. Nisibis, Edessa, Babylon-Seleucia, Ctesiphon

11. Herodian, III, 9, 12

## PART 3

# THE FORUM SINCE THE END OF ANTIQUITY

### CHAPTER 9
### THE DESTRUCTION OF THE FORUM

1. Cassiodorus, *Varia*, VII, 15; III, 9

2. Procopius, *Bellum Gothicum*, I, 26

3. Later it was called the Temple of Romulus, and then of Peace

4. E.g. S. Maria in Cannapara (later S. Maria delle Grazie) in the sw corner of the Basilica Julia (a few medieval arches remain). The Basilica Aemilia, known as the Old Mint (Zecca Vecchia) because of the molten coins found in its pavement, housed S. Giovanni Campo in its SE end.

5. Alcuin (tr. Eva M. Sanford)

6. S. Maria Nova has been more generally known as S. Francesca Romana since the early seventeenth century. S. Maria Antiqua was replaced in the thirteenth century by S. Maria Liberatrice, rebuilt in the eighteenth century and demolished in 1902

7. The present facade, behind the porch, was built in 1602

### CHAPTER 10
### THE REDISCOVERY OF THE FORUM

1. The Basilica was also admired by the architect of Pennsylvania Station, New York City, who used it as the model for the main waiting room

2. Obituary in *The Times* (1925). Boni also re-created the *viridarium* of Alessandro Farnese on the Palatine, with classical plants

### APPENDIX 1
### WHAT THE FORUM LOOKS LIKE

1. Blocks are visible below the Temples of Saturn and of Castor and Pollux, the Regia, the Basilicas Aemilia and Julia, etc.

2. Pliny the elder, *Historia Naturalis*, XXXV, 47, 166

### APPENDIX 2
### VANISHED MONUMENTS

1. *British Museum Catalogue, Coins of the Roman Empire*, I, p. 14, no. 77

2. Cf. Dio Cassius, LXII, 6, 2. Nero also wears the radiate crown of Apollo on his coins. This had previously appeared with posthumous heads of the deified Augustus

3. Dionysius of Halicarnassus, II, 50, 54

4. Livy, I, 36, 4f

5. Statius, *Silvae*, I, 1

6. Propertius, IV, 2, 3ff. (tr. S.G. Tremenheere)

7. Ibid, 22, 2

8. Sallust, *Bellum Catilinae*, XLVI, 5; XLIX, 4

9. M. Grant, *Roman Anniversary Issues*, pp. 43, 52ff.

10. Procopius, *Bellum Gothicum*, I, 25

11. Suetonius, *Nero*, 13

12. Livy, I, 19, 2

13. Dio, 54, 25 (11 BC), cf. M. Grant, op. cit., pp. 4f., *Roman Imperial Money*, pp. 220, 223

14. Horace, *Satires*, II, 3, 18, cf. Cicero, *Sixth Philippic*, V, 15; *De Officiis*, II, XXIV, 87

15. Livy, XLI, 27

16. Horace, *Epistles*, I, 1, 54

17. Cicero, *Pro Cluentio*, XXXIV, 93; *Pro Flacco*, XXVIII, 66; *Pro Sestio*, XV, 34; *Post Reditum*, XV, 13; *De Domo Sua*, XXI, 54

18. *British Museum Catalogue, Coins of the Roman Republic*, I, 3383

19. Cicero, *Pro Sestio*, VIII, 18; Ovid, *Remedia Amoris*, 561; Persius, IV, 49

# Acknowledgments

*Sources of Illustrations*

In addition to the photographs by Werner Forman we have made use of the following sources of illustrations, whose help and permission we gratefully acknowledge: Akademie der bildenden Künste, Vienna 104; Alinari 23, 39 (below left) 56, 95, 115 (above), 168, 186, 194, 195 (above and below); Anderson 200; Bristol City Art Gallery 185; City of Birmingham Art Gallery 205; Fototeca Unione and Dr E. Nash at the American Academy in Rome, 28, 72, 105, 112, 133, 134, 139, 146, 159, 210, 212 (left and right), 213, 215 (centre); John Freeman Ltd 201, 203; Giuseppe Gatteschi 46, 64, 76, 90, 99, 110, 115 (below), 147 (below), 154, 157 (above), 217 (above); Graphische Sammlung, Albertina, Vienna 100, 102; C. Hülsen 39 (above), 57, 82, 109, 118, 138 (right), 152 (below); E. Laurenti 94, 149; Louvre 204 (below); Minneapolis Institute of Arts 198, 199; Montreal Museum of Fine Arts 122; Museum of Fine Arts, Springfield, Mass. 196; National Trust, Stourhead, and the Courtauld Institute of Art 187.

*Literary Sources*

We gratefully acknowledge also the kind permission of the following sources of quotation: J.P.V.D. Balsdon and Bodley Head Publishers (*Roman Women*); B. Perrin and Heinemann Educational Books Ltd (*Plutarch's Lives*, Loeb edition); S.G. Tremenheere and John Menzies (London) Ltd (*The Elegies of Propertius*).

# Chronological Table

| THE MONARCHY | THE REPUBLIC | | THE EMPIRE | |
|---|---|---|---|---|
| (The names of kings are mythical or semi-legendary and their dates are traditional) | 509 | Fall of the Monarchy (traditional date) | BC 27–AD 14 | Augustus (formerly Octavian) |
| | 499 (or 496) | Battle of Lake Regillus against the Latins | AD 14–37 | Tiberius |
| | 451–450 | The Twelve Tables | 37–41 | Caligula (Gaius) |
| | 396 | Fall of Veii | 41–54 | Claudius |
| 753–716 BC Romulus | 390 (or 387) | Sack of Rome by the Gauls | 54–68 | Nero |
| 715–672 Numa Pompilius | 338 | Latin League dissolved | 68–69 | Galba |
| 672–640 Tullus Hostilius | 280–275 | War with Pyrrhus of Epirus | 69 | Otho, Vitellius |
| 640–616 Ancus Marcius | 264–241 | First Punic War | 69–79 | Vespasian |
| 616–578 Tarquinius Priscus | 218–201 | Second Punic War (Hannibal) | 79–81 | Titus |
| 578–534 Servius Tullius | | | 81–96 | Domitian |
| 534–510 Tarquinius Superbus | 168 | Defeat of Perseus at Pydna (Third Macedonian War) | 96–98 | Nerva |
| | | | 98–117 | Trajan |
| | 146 | Destruction of Carthage and Corinth | 117–138 | Hadrian |
| | | | 138–161 | Antoninus Pius |
| | 112–105 | War against Jugurtha of Numidia | 161–180 | Marcus Aurelius |
| | | | 180–192 | Commodus |
| | 81–79 | Dictatorship of Sulla after civil and eastern wars | 193–211 | Septimius Severus (after civil wars) |
| | 63 | Suppression of conspiracy of Catiline | 211–217 | Caracalla (Geta 211–212) |
| | | | 218–222 | Elagabalus |
| | 60 | First Triumvirate: Pompey, Crassus and Caesar | 238–244 | Gordian III |
| | | | 270–275 | Aurelian |
| | 58–51 | Caesar's Gallic War | 283–284 | Carinus |
| | 52 | Murder of Clodius | 284/6–305 | Diocletian and Maximian |
| | 48 | Battle of Pharsalus (Civil War between Caesar and Pompey) | 306–312 | Maxentius |
| | | | 306–337 | Constantine the Great |
| | 44 | Assassination of Caesar | 337–361 | Constantius II (at first reigning with his brothers) |
| | 43 | Second Triumvirate: Antony, Octavian, Lepidus. Death of Cicero | 361–363 | Julian 'the Apostate' |
| | | | 364–375 | Valentinian I |
| | | | 367–383 | Gratian |
| | 42 | Battle of Philippi and deaths of Brutus and Cassius | 375–392 | Valentinian II |
| | | | 392–394 | Eugenius |
| | 31 | Battle of Actium | 379–395 | Theodosius I |
| | 30 | Deaths of Antony and Cleopatra | 392–423 | Honorius |
| | | | 425–455 | Valentinian III |
| | | | 467–472 | Anthemius |
| | | | 475–493 | Romulus Augustulus: last emperor of the west |
| | | | 476–493 | Odoacer: king of Italy |
| | | | 493–518 | Theodoric: king of Italy |

# Some Books on the Forum

BARTOLI, A., *The Roman Forum : the Palatine*, Milan 1930

BRILLIANT, R., *The Arch of Septimius Severus in the Roman Forum (Memoirs of the American Academy in Rome*, xxix), Rome 1967

DUDLEY, D. R., *Urbs Roma*, Phaidon 1967

EGGER, H., *Römische Veduten*, Vienna 1931

GJERSTAD, E., *Early Rome* (Skrifter utgivna av Svenska Institutet i Rom, 4, XVII, i–iv, 2), Lund 1953–66

HARE, A., *Walks in Rome*, Routledge 1878

HOLZINGER, H., *The Museums and Ruins of Rome*, Vol. II *The Ruins*, Duckworth 1906

HUELSEN, C., *The Roman Forum*, London 1928

LANCIANI, R., *History of the Destruction of Ancient Rome*, London 1901, reprint 1969

LANCIANI, R., *The Roman Forum*, Rome 1910

LUGLI, G., *Monumenti Minori del Foro Romano*, Rome 1947

LUGLI, G., *Roma Antica : Il Centro Monumentale*, Rome 1946

LUGLI, G., *The Roman Forum and the Palatine*, Rome 1964

MARUCCHI, H., *Le Forum Romain et le Palatin d'après les dernières découvertes*, 2nd ed., Rome 1925 (English ed. 1906)

MASSON, G., *The Companion Guide to Rome*, Collins 1956

NASH, E., *Pictorial Dictionary of Ancient Rome*, new ed., Thames & Hudson 1968

PALMER, R.E.A., *The King and the Comitium*, Hermes-Einzelschrift 1969

PLATNER, S. B., and ASHBY, T., *A Topographical Dictionary of Ancient Rome*, O.U.P. 1929

ROMANELLI, P., *The Roman Forum*, 4th ed., Rome 1964

DE RUGGIERO, E., *Il Foro Romano*, Rome-Arpino 1913

SCHERER, M.R., *Marvels of Ancient Rome*, Phaidon 1955

THÉDÉNAT, H., *Le Forum Romain et les Forums Impériaux*, 5th ed., Paris 1911

WELIN, E., *Studien zur Topographie des Forum Romanum*, Lund 1953

# Hours of Opening

The archaeological site of the Forum Romanum and Palatine Hill is entered from the Via dei Fori Imperiali. It can also be reached, via the Palatine Hill, by the reconstructed Portale di Vignola in the Via di San Gregorio (and the gate-keeper will usually let one out, though not in, beside the Arch of Titus). The site is open during the months October–May from 9 a.m. until 5 p.m., and during the months June–September from 9 a.m. until 7 p.m. It is closed on Tuesdays.

In summer, there are evening performances of Son et Lumière in the Forum, and concerts can be heard in the Basilica of Maxentius.

The monuments beneath the foot of the Capitoline Hill (Temples of Vespasian and Concord, and Portico of the Twelve Gods) are not directly accessible but can be seen from the Via del Foro Romano.

Tabularium (Record Office): the gallery behind the arcade, containing architectural decoration from the Temples of Vespasian and Concord, can be visited from the Via del Campidoglio or Via di San Pietro in Carcere from 10 a.m. until 5 p.m. Closed Mondays. At the time of writing, the internal rooms and court of the Tabularium are inaccessible. The former can be glimpsed from inside the Palace of the Senator (Palazzo Senatorio, del Senatore) in the Piazza del Campidoglio, but this is not open to the public.

The Carcer Mamertinus (Tullianum, prison), 123 Via del Foro Romano, is open from 8 a.m. to 12 noon and from 2 p.m. until sunset.

The Forum Museum (Antiquarium Forense) – entrance inside the Forum site in 53 Piazza S. Maria Nova – is open from 9 a.m. until 1 p.m. Closed on Tuesdays.

The Antiquarium Comunale (Palazzo Caffarelli) is closed to the public, though special exhibitions of some of its contents have been given.

The Capitoline Museums (Museo Capitolino and Palazzo dei Conservatori, entrances in Piazza del Campidoglio, to left and right respectively after ascending the steps), are open from 9 a.m. until 2 p.m.; also on Tuesdays and Thursdays from 5 p.m. until 8 p.m. and on Saturdays also from 9 p.m. until 11.30 p.m. On public holidays from 9 a.m. until 1 p.m. Closed on Mondays.

The Museum of Roman Civilization (Museo della Civiltà Romana) contains a model of ancient Rome in imperial times, and includes reproductions of objects from the Forum. It is in the Piazza Agnelli in the EUR quarter (Esposizione Universale di Roma), south of Rome, and is open from 9 a.m. to 2 p.m.; also on Tuesdays and Thursdays during June–September from 5 p.m. to 8 p.m. Closed on Mondays and during August.

On civil or religious public holidays special enquiries should be made to discover whether sites and museums are open.

The times given here are not guaranteed. They are liable to be changed.

# Index